THE SHAAR PRESS

THE JUDAICA IMPRINT
FOR THOUGHTFUL PEOPLE

BIBLICAL
QUESTIONS

A
SHAAR
PRESS
PUBLICATION

SPIRITUAL
JOURNEYS

*Searching the Bible
for timely answers to eternal questions*

EMANUEL FELDMAN

Published by **SHAAR PRESS**
Distributed by MESORAH PUBLICATIONS, LTD.
4401 Second Avenue / Brooklyn, N.Y 11232 / (718) 921-9000 / www.artscroll.com

Distributed in Israel by SIFRIATI / A. GITLER
6 Hayarkon Street / Bnei Brak 51127

Distributed in Europe by LEHMANNS
Unit E, Viking Business Park, Rolling Mill Road / Jarrow, Tyne and Wear, NE32 3DP/ England

Distributed in Australia and New Zealand by GOLDS WORLD OF JUDAICA
3-13 William Street / Balaclava, Melbourne 3183 / Victoria Australia

Distributed in South Africa by KOLLEL BOOKSHOP
Shop 8A Norwood Hypermarket / Norwood 2196, Johannesburg, South Africa

ISBN: 1-57819-421-0 Hard Cover
ISBN: 1-57819-422-9 Paperback

Printed in the United States of America by Noble Book Press
Custom bound by Sefercraft, Inc. / 4401 Second Avenue / Brooklyn N.Y. 11232

For my wife —

and for our children,

their children,

and their children's children.

May their questions always be Biblical,

And their journeys always spiritual

OTHER BOOKS BY
EMANUEL FELDMAN

- ▸ *The 28th of Iyar*
- ▸ *Law as Theology*
- ▸ *The Biblical Echo*
- ▸ *On Judaism*
- ▸ *Tales Out of Shul*
- ▸ *One Plus One Equals One*
- ▸ *The Shul Without a Clock*

- ▸ Editor: *The Ariel Chumash*
- ▸ Editor: *Eis Ratzon:* a new translation of the Psalms
- ▸ Editor: Tradition Magazine (1989-2002)

TABLE OF CONTENTS

INTRODUCTION

A WISE MAN'S QUESTION
IS HALF THE ANSWER

The world is of the opinion
that the key to a good and blessed life
is to have good answers.
The world is mistaken.
The key to a good and blessed life
is to ask good questions.

So wrote an unknown Jewish sage of the Middle Ages, in words that resonate at full volume in contemporary times. The modern mind has little patience with questions. What matters are the answers. But we fail to understand that a good question, even when answered, never disappears; it remains in place, forever probing, goading, searching.

Especially is this true of the many questions found in the Bible, some of which are explored in this book. The purpose of Biblical questions is not simply to elicit a response. Rather, their purpose is to generate thought and reflection, and ultimately to remove the masks that so effectively cover our selves and our behavior. Biblical questions — such as *Where are you?* or *Where is your brother?* or *Am I my brother's keeper?* or *Who are you?* or *Why are you sad today?* — penetrate the calcified surfaces of our being and touch us at the core. Although they are addressed to specific Biblical person-alities, they are in actuality eternal questions addressed to everyone. They endure and abide, transcending time and place.

A spiritual journey of a thousand miles begins with one good Biblical question. To listen carefully to that question, to consider its multi-layered meanings, is to set out on an exciting voyage of explo-ration and discovery. This is why it is a Jewish maxim that *sh'eilat chacham chatzi teshuvah/*"a wise man's question is half the answer."

In my own journey of discovery in writing this book I have had the invaluable assistance of many people. My wife, Estelle, with her unerring eye for precise expression and her finely honed sense of style, has been a constant and faithful editor. My brother, HaRav Aharon Feldman, has taken precious time from his own heavy schedule as Rosh HaYeshivah of Ner Israel to share with me his scholarship and wisdom. I have also benefited immeasurably from conversations with (alphabetically) our son Rabbi Ilan Daniel Feldman of Atlanta; Rabbi Hillel Goldberg of Denver; Rabbi Matis Greenblatt of Jerusalem; Mr. Yosef HaKohen of Jerusalem; Rabbi Leib Hyman of Jerusalem; Prof. William Kolbrener of Bar Ilan University. Each of them has graciously read parts of the manu-script and made perceptive and useful suggestions. ArtScroll's Rabbi Nosson Scherman has been a vigilant and sensitive editor whose learning and insights have enhanced the manuscript from beginning to end. Obviously, I retain exclusive rights to any errors of commission or omission, and share them with no one else.

I offer thanks to the One Above Who has preserved me in life and allowed me to complete this book about His Book. May the material presented here serve to deepen our understanding of the Biblical text, and help enhance our relationship to the other beside us and to the Other above us. And may our ears remain open to the good questions.

— Emanuel Feldman
Jerusalem
28 Menahem Av, 5764/August 2004

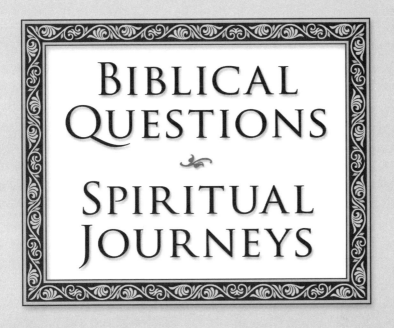

BIBLICAL QUESTIONS

SPIRITUAL JOURNEYS

IN QUEST
OF THE BIBLICAL QUESTION

✒ *The Question as Statement*

It is a curious phenomenon of the Biblical text that instead of using simple declarative sentences, the Bible frequently uses the question form. The book of Genesis alone contains hundreds of questions of all kinds, and the one hundred-fifty chapters of the Psalms contain almost ninety questions.

We list some examples below. The straightforward declarative sentence — which the Bible might have used but does not — is shown first, followed by the actual Biblical use of the identical idea in the form of a question, which is italicized:

▸ Cain to God: I am not my brother's keeper.
  Torah text: Am I my brother's keeper? (Genesis 4:9)

▸ Abraham to God: The Divine Judge will surely do justice.
  Will the Divine Judge not do justice? (ibid. 18:25)

▸ Judah to his brothers: There is no profit in killing him.
  What does it profit us to kill him? (ibid. 37:26)

▸ Joseph to his brothers: I am not in place of God.
  Am I in place of God? (ibid. 50:19)

- The Israelites to Moses: There are many graves in Egypt. *Is there a lack of graves in Egypt?* (Exodus 14:11)
- *Israel to God at the Red Sea:* No one is like You, O God. *Who is like You, O God?* (ibid. 15:11)
- Moses and Micah: This is what the Lord requires of you. *What does the Lord ask of you?* (Deuteronomy 10:12) *What does the Lord require of you?* (Micah 6:8)
- God to Israel: Your fathers have found no iniquity in Me …. *What iniquity have your fathers found in Me that they have distanced themselves from Me?* (Jeremiah 2:5)
- King David cries out to God: You have forsaken me. *Why have you forsaken me?* (Psalms 22:2)
- The Jews to their captors: We cannot sing God's song in the land of the stranger. *How can we sing God's song in the land of the stranger?* (Ibid. 137:4)
- God to Job: You cannot dispatch lightning … *Can you dispatch lightning bolts?* (Job 38:35)

There are many more examples. (Who can count the numerous examples?) Some, as we have seen in this sampling, are rhetorical: a verbal answer is obvious and is not sought. What is sought is a non-verbal reply: full agreement with the idea expressed in the question.

But Biblical questions are rich, subtle, and variegated, and go far beyond the classic rhetorical type. Even the ordinary questions which seem to request information are seen, upon examination, to be much more than that. Thus, when God asks Adam, "Where are you?" or asks Cain, "Where is your brother?" He obviously knows the answer, but nevertheless chooses to approach His subject through the vehicle of a question. It is equally clear that in questions such as these, a far wider audience is being addressed, one which extends beyond the immediate confines of the question.

That is to say, many apparently innocent Biblical questions are more than isolated, local inquiries. Instead they sound a universal echo. Certain questions like "Who am I?" or "Who are you?" ripple out into much wider circles than the literal words that contain them. They transcend their immediate textual context and cascade into much larger meanings that are designed to challenge and to discomfit, to uncover and to discover.

Man is a questioning creature, and the Torah is a questioning book. When the text asks "Who?", and "Why?", "What?", "Where?", and "When?", it reflects the essential nature of Adam, who is the prototype of a humanity that is curious, that probes, that seeks to uncover and discover (an exemplary trait — but one that, if left unchecked, can lead to sinful fruit). It is instructive that the Hebrew letters for Adam (*aleph, daled, mem*) have the numerical equivalent of 45, and the Hebrew letters for the most widely used Hebrew interrogative, *mah* ["what?"] (*mem, heh*) also have the sum of 45. This is no coincidence, for Adam is the embodiment of he-who-seeks, he-who-inquires.

This predilection for the question is most apparent in the Biblical injunctions concerning the Pesach offering and in the Pesach Seder itself. The Torah's account begins with a question: *ki yish'alcha bincha, mah zot?* — "When your son will ask you, what is this...?" (Deuteronomy 6:20). The Torah does not use the words "*if* your son will ask," but rather, "*when* your son will ask." Asking questions is an integral element in the transmission of the Torah tradition.

In this spirit, the Pesach Seder and its Haggadah are centered on the questions of the Four Sons, and on the Four Questions which the child at the Seder asks his father. So essential is the question-and-answer format that even if someone conducts the Pesach Seder alone he is required to ask the four questions of himself and to respond to them himself (*Pesachim* 116a).

It is significant that the awe and wonder of the great transforming events in sacred history are phrased in questions, as in the Exodus, noted above, and at the Revelation at Sinai (Deuteronomy 4:32-34):

*For **ask** now ... has there ever been anything like this great thing, or has anything like it been heard? Has a people ever heard the voice of God speaking from the midst of the fire? ... has God ever come to take for Himself a nation from the midst of another nation?*

This distinctive characteristic of Torah is carried over into the Oral Torah as well. Question and answer, contradiction and reconciliation, puzzlement and resolution, relentless probing and inquiry: these are the bricks and mortar of Talmudic methodology.

There is something in the nature of a question that is more potent than an ordinary sentence. Clearly, the impact upon someone who hears a question is greater than the impact upon someone who hears a straightforward sentence. In the list of examples cited above, it is apparent that the form of the question — in every case — is far more powerful than the statement expressing the very same idea.

Could the force and impact that is inherent in a question have been the motivation for Targum Onkelos's unusual translation of Genesis 18:25? Abraham, in an attempt to save Sodom, says to God, "Shall the Judge of all the earth not exercise justice?" The Hebrew text is clearly in the form of a challenging interrogative. But Onkelos translates this not as a question but as a statement: "The Judge of all the earth shall indeed do justice." Onkelos may feel that the question is much too forceful and too bold to be addressed to God, and so he softens it by rendering it as an indicative sentence.

What are the elements within a question that make it such an effective means of communication? For one thing, a declarative sentence, once it is completed, evaporates. It comes to an end at the closing period. It states its business, makes its case, and then moves on.

Not so the question. It does not evaporate. The question engages, holding the listener by the lapel, drawing him close. It is the opening of a dialogue. In Deuteronomy, Chapter 1, Moses twice refers to the burdens of leadership. In verse 9 he expresses it in a straightforward sentence: "I am not able to bear you myself alone." In verse 12 he utters almost the identical words, but this time as a question: *Eichah?* — "How can I bear alone your cumbrance and your burden and your strife?"

It is obvious which is the more compelling of the two.

Unlike the garden variety statement, the question knows no boundaries and has no limits. It does not end at the question mark. On the contrary, that mark is the springboard from which the question leaps into the air, remaining there, awaiting some response. And even when there is no response, or when no response is expected — as in a rhetorical question — the question does not vanish: the issue raised by the question continues to hover in the atmosphere — reproaching, lamenting, pleading, defying, or persuading.

Thus, the question penetrates the mind of the listener as a statement cannot. Even a rhetorical question transforms the monologue of a statement into a dialogue between two people. He to whom a question is addressed knows that his participation is sought. One can ignore a statement; it is much more difficult to ignore a question. Thus, a person contemplating a rose might say to his companion, "This is an exquisite rose." Alternatively, he might ask, "Is not this a beautiful rose?" In the first instance, the speaker is expressing a personal opinion which the companion can accept or ignore. In the second instance, the speaker is inviting his companion to share in the experience of the rose, to agree or disagree, or, at the very least, to think about it.

Thus the heathen prophet Bilaam might have said, "No one can count the dust of Jacob." Instead, he asks, "Who can count the dust of Jacob?" (Numbers 23:20). The message of the statement and that of the question are identical: no one can count the dust, for it is limitless. But the message has infinitely more power when formulated as a question — because he who hears it is now forced to think of a possible answer, to reflect, and then to conclude that the answer is, "Indeed, no one."

Of the hundreds of questions that mark the Biblical landscape, I have plucked out only a handful for closer examination here. The criterion for their inclusion is straightforward: Those questions that speak most pointedly — and, occasionally, poignantly — to the Jewish and the human condition were the prime candidates. To be sure, most Biblical questions easily meet this criterion, but those I finally chose seemed to me to address most incisively some of the major issues of contemporary Jewish life: man's personal identity and his place in the universe; his relationship to the other beside him and to the Other above him; the definition and implications of sin; the meaning of suffering; pride and humility; the mysteries of Divine reward and punishment; the role of the Holy Land.

Although our discussions of the individual questions follow chronologically their appearance in the Biblical books, the chapters need not be read in the order in which they appear here. While there is a visible thread binding them all together, each chapter can stand on its own.

I am hopeful that readers will come away from this book with a deepened and sharpened understanding of some of the vital motifs within the Biblical/Judaic approach to human life.

Let us proceed. Better still: Shall we proceed?

2

... and she took from its fruit and ate; and she gave also to her husband and he ate ... They heard the voice of God manifesting itself in the Garden .... And the man and his wife hid from God .... God called out to the man and said to him: "Where are you?"

                                                                              Genesis 3:6-9

THE FOUNTAINHEAD OF LAMENT: GOD'S FIRST QUESTION TO ADAM: "WHERE ARE YOU?"

Adam, the climax of God's creation, he for whom the entire universe was created, for whom the dry land was separated from the waters, for whom the fish and the animals were formed, for whom the sun and the moon and the stars and the firmament were set into place, for whom all the creatures and the fruit and the vegetation, were placed upon the earth, for whom the wondrous universe was designed, who was set into the paradise of Eden — Adam is hiding, cringing, filled with guilt and shame and fear. God's own handiwork is hiding from Him who formed him in the Garden of Eden.

Ayekah, God asks. "Where are you?"

An odd question. God the Creator, the omniscient One, asks his lowly creature where he is. Why does He not simply order him to come forward? *Adam, stop cowering under that bush. Foolish creature of Mine, do you really think you can hide from Me? Adam, step forward!*

But God does not utter the command. Rather than confront His creation with His command, He introduces the subject with "Where are you?" — on the surface an innocent, innocuous question that gives Adam a chance to explain himself.

But on a deeper level, "Where are you?" is more than an inquiry about a location. It can also mean, *Why are you hiding? You heard Me walking in the Garden. Why do you not come forward to greet Me, your Creator, the One Who fashioned you? This is most strange: the creature I created and to whom I have given so much, attempts to conceal himself from Me, to avoid My presence!"*

Adam responds, apparently without guile: "I heard Your voice in the Garden; and I feared, because I am naked, and I hid myself" (Genesis 3:10).

This appears to be a straightforward response, but upon closer examination it is clear that Adam is not answering the question. God had asked, "Where are you?" Adam does not say where he is. He does not say, "I am here." Instead he explains why he tried to hide. Clearly, he understands the question on its deeper level. Not only, "Where are you hiding?", but more importantly, "*Why* are you hiding?"

But even with this reading, one word is still off-key. Instead of the word "feared," one would expect to find the word "ashamed": "I was ashamed, because I was naked, so I hid." This would have provided a certain symmetry to the text, echoing the similar term used earlier in 2:25: "and the two of them were naked and they were not ashamed."

Furthermore, at this point Adam was not naked at all. He and Eve had already covered themselves with fig leaves, immediately after they had eaten of fruit of the forbidden tree and first became aware of their nakedness (ibid. 3:7).

Adam's use of "fear" suggests that he is fully aware that he has violated the one commandment that he has been given. The entire Garden was permissible to him; no restrictions whatsoever were placed upon him — with a single exception: "From the tree of the knowledge of good and evil you shall not eat ...." (ibid. 1:17).

But even that one restriction was not observed. Adam and his mate Eve succumbed to the irresistible attraction of the forbidden, the overwhelming temptation of the illicit. And now, confronted and questioned by God, it is not his nakedness that preoccupies Adam, but his fear.

Perhaps Adam refers to a different kind of nakedness: not a nakedness of the flesh but of the spirit, the kind that encompasses one who turns his back on God and willfully violates His commandment. Having defied God, having turned away from his Creator, he stands stripped of His glory, bereft of His Divine light; he is desolate, alone, exposed, uncovered. This is the true nakedness. "I was afraid because I am naked, so I hid."

God's questions now come cascading down in a torrent: Two questions to Adam:

1) "Who told you that you were naked?"

2) "Have you eaten of the tree from which I commanded you not to eat?"

And one question to Eve:

"What is this that you have done?" (God will ask almost the identical question of Cain after he kills Abel: "What have you done?" (ibid. 4:10), and it will be heard repeatedly throughout the Bible, as will be seen in our detailed discussion of God's question to Eve.)

God knows the answers to all the questions. He knows where Adam is hiding, He knows how Adam discovered his nakedness, He knows that he ate from the tree, He knows what Eve has done. Why, then, the inquiry?

Because the purpose of the questions is not to seek answers. The purpose of the questions is to cause those who are questioned to pause, to think, to consider. For a question penetrates as a statement cannot. A question calls for an answer, and an answer requires reflection.

Especially the questions of God to man:

Where are you?

Are you bereft of God's glory, stripped of human dignity?

Have you obeyed My commandment, I Who created you to tower majestically over all My creatures? Or have you, like the beasts over whom you were to reign, fallen into the lure of your desires — and then tried to cover up and to hide?

Do you realize what you have done to your connection with Me; do you know what you have done to yourself?

Where were you yesterday, before you defied me? Where are you today, after your defiance? And where will you be tomorrow?

The question is not answered. But there is no such thing as an unanswered question from God. The letters that form the word of God's unanswered question, *Ayekah*, — the letters *Aleph, Yud, Kof,* and *Hei* — do not evaporate. They remain in the air, hovering and unfulfilled. And in time the hovering letters transmute themselves into a different word entirely, a word bearing the identical Hebrew letters. Now, however, they are no longer a question but a lament: God's *Ayekah* in Genesis becomes the *Eichah* of Moses crying out to God (Numbers 11:11): *"Eichah"* — Woe, How, Wherefore, Why — "How can I alone bear the burden of this difficult people?" And Jeremiah's book of *Lamentations* begins with this very word: *Eichah*: "Woe, the city sits solitary ...." and is repeated like a wail throughout the book.

Eichah, the most melancholy word in the Bible, rippling out of its brief two-syllableness into ever-widening circles of gloom and sorrow. The guttural groan of heartache, the inconsolable moan of *Eichah*:

How did this come about?

How could it happen?

How can this be?

Why is it so?

Woe.

Hidden in the crevices of the unanswered Where-are-you, its bitter fruit beginning to bud, is the sigh of Woe and Wherefore. Slowly gnawing away within the being of him who turns away and tries to hide is the muffled cry of lament.

Where-are-you is not a spatial, geographic inquiry. It is an existential question:

Where are you spiritually, intellectually, emotionally, now that you have moved away from Me?

Adam hiding, stooped, bent over, frightened, ashamed: do you really believe that I Who formed the eye cannot see you?

Or is it yourself from whom you are hiding?

Are you more content now than before you rebelled?

The ultimate question of God to man: *Ayekah?* "Where are you?"

The ultimate lament of man to God: *Eichah.* "Woe."

The path that ends with *Eichah* begins with *Ayekah.*

The geographical Where-are-you does not stand still.

It becomes the existential "Why," and the wondering "How," the inconsolable weep of woe and lamentation and grieving. Slowly gnawing away within the being of him who tries to hide from his Maker is the bitter groaning of lament. He who searches for the fountainhead of all lament will find it in the seed of turning away and hiding.

Where-are-you is not a spatial, geographic inquiry. It is an existential question about the essence of a person, a challenge to him.

God knows exactly where man is. But God wants man to ask the question of himself: Where am I?

Now that I have strayed from God, where am I now, and where was I before I sinned?

Where was I yesterday, where am I today, and where will I be tomorrow?

Am I more content now than I was before I rebelled?

Adam hiding, stooped, bent over, frightened:
Do you really believe that I Who formed the eye cannot see you?
Or is it yourself from whom you are hiding?

And Adam said: The woman whom you gave me, she gave me of the tree, and I ate. And the Lord God said to the woman: What is this that you have done?

Genesis 3:12-13

THE ANATOMY OF SIN. GOD'S FIRST QUESTION TO EVE: *WHAT HAVE YOU DONE?*

The first question of God to Adam, as we have seen, is Ayekah, *"Where are you?" The first question of God to Eve is* Mah zot asit, *"What is this that you have you done?" We have discussed the wider implications of "Where are you?" The question to Eve, "What have you done?" is the first of numerous such questions that God asks His creatures throughout the Bible. It is an eternal question, one that every honest human being must ask himself every day.*

Just as Adam and Eve prefigure the mankind that is to follow them, so also is their violation of the command of God a prefiguring of every transgression that is to follow it. Just as every human being born after Adam and Eve contains something of their genetic code within him, so does every sin committed since that first one contain an element of the genetic code of that very first sin.

What are the elements that constitute that first sin? Upon examination, they are seen to consist of temptation, rationalization, and self-justification — all accompanied by the loss of mastery over one's self.

I. A careful analysis of that very first sin yields some illuminating insights.

The serpent — the embodiment of temptation — tries to entice Eve into violating God's commandment. But he does so cleverly and subtly. Although Eve protests that God has forbidden them to "eat of the tree nor to touch it lest they die" (Genesis 3:3), the serpent realizes that she has added her own restriction, and that there is no restriction against touching the tree, only against eating its fruit. (See *Sanhedrin 29a; Midrash Bereshit Rabbah 19:3.*) Whereupon the serpent gently persuades Eve to brush against the forbidden tree. When she remains unharmed, the serpent assures her that just as she did not die from touching it, so will she not die if she eats from it: "The serpent said to the woman, You will surely not die" (Genesis 3:4). You have been forbidden to eat from it because God is afraid that once you and Adam eat from it, "you will be like God, knowing good and evil" (ibid. 3:5).

Eve apparently finds the serpent's words eminently reasonable and persuasive. *Why else would God forbid that fruit? There must be some hidden motive in that prohibition. It is in God's self-interest to forbid it, but it is not in our self-interest. The serpent is right. Just as no harm befell me when I touched it, so will I not die if I eat it; and when I do eat it, I will be as great as God Himself.*

And now she begins to see the tree from a different perspective entirely. The fruit has suddenly become desirable, tantalizing, irresistible. Read the words in verse 6 very carefully, for in these 21 Hebrew words lie the key to the understanding of what transpired at that very first sin:

And the woman perceived that the tree was good for eat-
ing, and that it was a delight [taavah — which can also be
"desire"] to the eyes, and that the tree was desirable as a
means to wisdom, and she took of its fruit and ate, and
she gave also to her husband with her and he ate.

This is what emerges from this verse:
1) The fruit is delicious.
2) It offers obvious delight and pleasure.
3) It is desirable, for it makes one wise

That is to say, the forbidden fruit appeals 1) to the Physical self (delicious); 2) to the Emotional self (delight, desire); and 3) to the Intellectual self (wise).

Eve had not perceived all this before. But now that that she is in the grip of temptation, the fruit, which she had earlier avoided, now becomes the most important object in her life, something that she absolutely must possess. In a word, she lusts for it, and her lust is rationalized on the physical, the emotional, and the intellectual levels. Her need for it is overpowering, shutting off her rational mind to the inconvenient fact that her Creator has forbidden it. *No matter. It is delicious, it is filled with delight, it offers me the kind of pleasure I have never had, and it will make me as wise as God. On all counts I must possess it immediately — now, without delay.*

Note that between her desire for it and her eating of it there is no time lapse. It all takes place in the same verse. There is no pause, even for breath, between "The tree was desirable" and "she took of its fruit …." Note also the speed with which her attitude changes. One verse earlier she had declared that it was forbidden, and then, upon hearing a reason as to why it ought not be forbidden, she immediately falls captive to the power of the sin.

Question: how can she know the fruit is delicious when she has not yet tasted it? Such, however, is the power of illicit craving. She is no longer in command, no longer at the helm. The object of her desire has taken over. So compelling is the passion that is driving her that it is as if she has already tasted it.

Here we have the anatomy of sin. In this one resonant verse, the Torah demonstrates how Eve loses mastery of herself and how the transgression overpowers her. The forbidden fruit has become the captor, and she has become its captive.

We find here a primary cause of sin: the intrusion of our own rational faculties. Ideally, the commandment of God is to be performed for no other reason than that it is the will of God. Even if we discover a rational basis for the command, it is to be performed as if there were no rational basis for it. Just as God does not offer Adam any reasons that the tree is forbidden, so also are the overwhelming majority of the later commandments of the Torah given without reasons. We are not told to maintain Kashruth laws because they are hygienic, or to observe the Shabbat because it is good for us to rest once a week, or to practice circumcision because of health considerations. All these reasons could be true, but they are not the reason for our performance of the commandments.

An illuminating insight on this matter is offered by the Talmud: Only two Biblical commandments — the restrictions on an Israelite king regarding having too many wives or horses — were recorded with their reasons: lest the wives cause his heart to "go astray," and lest the horses cause him "to return to Egypt" (see Deuteronomy 17:16-17). The Sages comment that precisely because these reasons were given, "the greatest in the world [Solomon] was caused to stumble." He violated these laws because he was convinced that such fears did not apply to him: his heart would not go astray and he would not return to Egypt (*Sanhedrin* 21b).

It is not easy to live up to the idealized portrait of the true servant of God who serves his Master without knowing or requiring any reasons. The great Rabbeinu Nissim Gerondi (1310–1375) in his comments to *Kiddushin* 31a, suggests that human nature is innately rebellious and tends to resist authority and flout commandments, and that therefore he who serves God not because of reason but because it is God's command is the true servant of God, having overcome his inborn predilection to be disobedient. (See his *Derashot HaRan HaShalem* [Mossad HaRav Kook, 2003] *D'rush*

Hashvi'i, p. 265 ff.) This is not to suggest that there is anything rebellious behind the strong impulse to try to plumb the rationale that purportedly lies behind the commandments of God. There is in fact a vast corpus of classical literature in Judaism that deals with *taamei hamitzvot,* "reasons for the mitzvot." But this literature has an underlying motif: that God is to be served even when no adequate reason is discovered.

The inappropriate use of one's rational faculties is a universal problem when it comes to Divine service. Thus, King Saul's violation of the command to destroy Amalek is also based on such inappropriate use. Saul erroneously deduced from the laws of the *Eglah Arufah*, the "Decapitated Calf" (Deuteronomy 21:1-9) — in which a great tumult is made about the death of one person — that God surely did not mean for him to destroy all of Amalek. But because he spared Amalek in violation of the Divine command, he lost his kingship (I Samuel 15). Of Saul it was said that "whoever is merciful when he should be unmerciful, will end up being unmerciful when he should be merciful" — referring to Saul's destruction of Nob, the city of Kohanim (*Yoma* 22b; *Kohelet Rabbah* 7:16).

So it is with Eve. She is persuaded by the purported rationale behind the commandment — God is fearful that you will become like gods — and she finds immediate cause to ignore it. Once a reason is given for a commandment, inevitably there emerges a parallel reason why the command should not be performed. The reason behind it is unfair; the reason does not apply to me; or the reason makes no sense. This is why Judaism has always felt that while it is good to probe and to inquire and to try to comprehend, man must know that ultimately his mortal and fallible reason cannot hope to fathom the vast depths that lie beneath the commandments of the immortal and infallible God. For believers, reasons are not necessary; for non-believers, reasons are of no avail.

That Eve's fall is so swift is prototypical of the sinner. The temptation to violate God's law is ever present, and the human being is ever at risk of stumbling into its grasp. As God will say later to Cain, "Sin crouches at the door" (Genesis 4:7).

Enter into this scene the voice of God: *Mah zot asit?* "What is this that you have done?"

II. This first *What have you done?* in the Bible is to be followed by many others, for in every sin that man will ever commit, these same elements will play the major role.

Thus God confronts Cain after he murders his brother: *Mah asita?* "What have you done?" (Genesis 4:10).

Similarly, Joshua confronts Achan about his violation of the edict not to take spoils from Jericho: *Meh asita?* "What have you done?" (Joshua 7:19).

Yet again, we find Samuel confronting King Saul after Saul defies the commandment of God: *Mah asita?* "What have you done?" (I Samuel 13:11).

What have you done? This is not simply a cry of exasperation from a mother to her child who has just dirtied the carpet. That mother's exclamation does not require any response. But when God asks Eve what she has done, He does expect her to respond. He is informing her that she must consider to the full what specifically she has done, and must contemplate its implications. The question is a rebuke to her, as it is to every sinner, in that she is obligated to be conscious of and aware of the consequences of her deeds.

An act that violates God's explicit command cannot be committed and then forgotten. Such an act — a transgression — does not come to an end. It resonates beyond the moment of the sin. It does not evaporate or vanish into thin air. Its contaminating effects hang on.

When a person violates God's commandment, he has not only done something against the will of God; he has also done something to society, to his relationship with God, to God's world, and to himself. The sin is thus not an isolated act perpetrated in a cocoon. Like a contagious disease, it affects, and infects, not only the sinner, but everyone around him — for immediately Eve gives of the forbidden fruit to Adam and he also eats.

In fact, a sinner causes everyone within the community to taste an infinitesmal portion of the forbidden fruit — including even those who strive to create a close relationship with God through the performance of mitzvos and the study of sacred texts, and who engage in acts of prayer, lovingkindness, and charity. His actions cast a pall of resentment, disappointment, and discouragement over everyone in his surroundings, thereby weakening the resolve of those who would reach out to their Creator in purity.

Furthermore, even if he does not view his private sin in such cosmic terms, the sinner has in effect mounted an assault on God's architecture of the universe. For just as there is design in the physical elements of the universe, so is there design in its spiritual elements. The details of that design are found in the mitzvos of the Torah. Since we are partners with God in building and maintaining His world, each individual act of obedience to the Divine command reinforces the supporting beams of the Divine edifice and continues to build the structure of the universe; conversely, each individual rebellion against His command undermines those beams, tears them down, and thus affects the integrity of the entire structure.

A sin has staying power; it continues to have its effects in ever widening circles. Not the least of these is the new condition which it now creates within the sinner himself. Before a person commits his first sin, it is off limits, out of the question, forbidden. But once the sin has been committed, once it has been granted entry into the house and becomes a guest within its walls — once it has gained entrance into the human heart — it is very difficult to dislodge it. It insinuates itself into the person's consciousness, then ingratiates itself, and soon it becomes much easier to sin again, for the innate purity of the soul has been sullied. So persuasive is the power of sin, so potent is the human ability to justify and to rationalize one's every action, that after the sin is committed again and again, the sin somehow ceases to be something that is wrong and becomes transmogrified into a positive good (cf. *Sotah* 22a).

Mah zot asit? "What is this that you have done?" The question is a call to think and to consider. Better to consider before the act — but if the sin has already been committed, it is still not too late to consider what has been done, so that a second and a third sin might be prevented. Obviously, however, *"What am I about to do?"* — to think before one acts, to consider the consequences of this moment of fleeting pleasure — is much more effective than "What have I done?" — after the act. In the words of Pirke Avot (2:1): a person is advised to weigh what he will gain by the sin against what he will lose: *Hevai mechashev hefsed mitzvah k'neged secharah, u'schar aveirah k'neged hefsedah* / "Calculate the cost of a mitzvah against its reward, and the reward of a sin against its cost." A person is advised to weigh what he will gain by the sin against what he will lose. (See also *Bava Batra* 78b.)

In brief, what have you done — to yourself? What have you gained by this act of yours. Look carefully at what exactly you have achieved. If you have stolen, you have gained money or possessions, but you have distanced yourself from your Maker. What have you done? If you have killed, you have had only a momentary release from your rage, but in so doing you have snuffed out the life of a human being, a creature of God. If you have committed adultery, you have had a momentary excitement which has long since disappeared. If you have destroyed someone's reputation by gossip, what have you gained by this? If you violated any mitzvah deliberately, you have in effect behaved as if God were not present, and by so doing you have made it even more difficult to knock at His door in the future — unless you acknowledge what you have done, turn back towards God through the process of genuine repentance known as *teshuvah,* and become as a cleansed, newborn person once again.

Even what may seem like an innocuous sin — and no sin against God is truly innocuous — has the power to block God's radiance from the sinner. The great teacher of Mussar, the "Alter of Kelm" (Rabbi Simcha Z. Ziv, 1849–1919), suggests that just as a flimsy slip of paper can shield one from the blinding rays of the sun, so also any deliberate sin, no matter how slight it may seem, has the power to block out the radiance of God Himself. The prophet Isaiah phrases it this way: "Your transgressions have caused Him to hide His countenance from you" (Isaiah 59:2). (See *Daat Torah*, by R. Yerucham Levovitz, vol. I, p. 82 [Jerusalem, 5736].)

Granted, when a man is caught up in the grip of sin, his rational, intellectual faculties often cease functioning, and the question, "*What am I about to do?*", is quickly dispatched under a barrage of self-justification and immediate gratification. Nevertheless, the "*What have you done?*" that he hears after the deed can at the very least prod the sinner to ask himself why he did what he did, and it can make him aware, in the midst of his self-justification, of the serious ramifications of his act.

Of course, the sinner might well respond, "*I did nothing. I lost control. I had no intention to rebel against God's will. It was an accident. I was forced into it. I wasn't thinking. I know now that it was wrong.*"

Well and good. Certainly an inadvertent violation of God's will is not as serious as a deliberate one, for it is not a rebellion *per se* against God's authority. Nevertheless, "I had no intention" is not an adequate defense. A human being is a thinking creature, and he cannot simply wipe away his deeds by saying, "I did not know what I was doing," or "I did not mean any harm." During the Temple's existence, even an unintentional sin, one committed in ignorance or in error — *beshogeg* — nevertheless obligated the sinner to bring a sin-offering called a *chatat*. Why an offering when the sin was inadvertent? Because a Jew is obligated to think and to consider, and not to act out of instinct or habit or anger. He is obligated to be constantly aware of the Presence of God and of the pervasive presence of His commandments. *Thinking man does not act inadvertently.* (See *Sotah* 32b concerning the shame that is associated even with an accidental transgression.)

It is true that once he is in the grip of sin, a person is not fully conscious of his actions. The Sages say: "When a soul sins, a spirit of folly and madness enters him" (*Sotah* 3a). They mean that no fully sane person who is aware of the obvious Presence of the Creator of the universe, could deliberately and consciously violate His commandment. A temporary madness overcomes him and he follows his instincts instead of his reason — literally losing his mind. The madness may be in the form of self-justification: I need this item more than the owner; he is rich and will never miss it. Or the madness is in the form of passion, anger, or lust which mutiny within him and wrest away the controls of his life.

But the folly or madness defense does not absolve the sinner. It is a description of the process of sinning; it is not a justification for sinning. The sinner remains responsible for his actions.

III. Thus, there are three elements in *Meh asita? "What have you done?"*

A) *What?* The classic Biblical question-word, *mah* (or *meh*) — found over ninety times in Genesis alone — is a challenge hurled at the sinner. Having done what he wishes, having followed his own impulse, he is by now very likely justifying his action, and might even be considering a repeat performance. But the one-syllable word *mah* pulls him up short: *What?* With this question suddenly before him, the sinner finds himself confronted by someone who is scrutinizing his deed. The question is an accusing finger. "*What have you done?*" Its very directness penetrates his being and echoes and reverberates within him, creating doubts and second thoughts. At the peak of his satisfaction at having pulled off his personal rebellion against authority comes the "*mah.*" His action is being questioned, his deed is being doubted. *What I did felt so right. Is it possible that it was wrong?* A huge question mark has been placed at his feet. Having heard the querying *mah,* inner qualms begin to gnaw away at him. He was so certain that this deed had to be done, just as Eve had no question about her overpowering need for the overpowering fruit. But now he is not so certain.

This little question-word, *mah,* might be one of the most potent words in the entire Bible. Its two Hebrew letters possess the ability to challenge and to create doubt in the most self-righteous of transgressors.

B) *You.* There is no other perpetrator of this act but *you.* You cannot blame anyone else. *You* must take responsbility for it. It is no defense to claim that "he" or "she" or "my parents" or "my upbringing" or "my environment" or "society" did it. You performed the act. You are responsible. You must rectify it. If it is a sin against another human being, you rectify it by asking his forgiveness and, where applicable, compensating him for the damage or returning what you stole; if it is against God, you rectify it by genuine contrition and the process of penitence, *teshuvah.*

Granted, it is natural to attempt to place the onus upon others. When confronted by God, Adam blames Eve. Eve then blames the serpent. While God does punish the serpent for inciting Eve, and he punishes Adam for falling prey to the blandishments of Eve, God holds Eve responsible, for, after all, it was she who first committed the act of rebellion against Him. She is the perpetrator of the deed. The responsibility for the destruction of God's plan for mankind rests primarily in her hands. Therefore God asks *Mah zot asit* of her alone, and He does not ask it of Adam or of the serpent.

C) *Done.* This is the key word. In Hebrew, an active, not a passive verb: *"asita,"* literally "you did." It is insufficient to say that somehow a violation of God's will took place — passively. Not at all: *asita,* you yourself did it. You performed a deed, you effected an action. You did it in real time, in the real world. It is not only that something was stolen, but you stole; not only that something evil was spoken, but you spoke it; not only that a mitzvah was violated, but you violated it.

There is one positive aspect to *"asit"*: it is in the past tense — "done." It took place in the past; it is no longer taking place now, and perhaps it will not be repeated in the future. Hopefully it is finished, completed, literally "done."

IV. We have seen the effects of sin on the sinner's surroundings, on his relationship to God, on God's ultimate design for the world, and on the sinner himself. But there remains yet one additional consequence of that very first rebellion against Divine authority: When Adam and Eve sinned, death entered the world in the wake of that sin.

Death is generally viewed as a punishment for their sin, but it is more than that. It is not quite true that the wages of sin is death, which means that death is the result of sin. Rather, sin itself is a form of death. When a person sins, he rejects the authority of the Creator Who is the God of Life. For no less than five times is God referred to in the Bible as *Elo-him Chaim,* "Living God," and as *El Chai* eight times. The most widely used oath in the Bible is that which swears by the "livingness of God," which is found over thirty-six times. And God swears by His own livingness — *chai Ani* — over seventeen times. In the process of turning his back on this God of life, something living within the sinner withers away, and death enters his being. This is because God is the God of life, and death is the opposite of life. When the sinner chooses to reject God's sovereignty over him, he has chosen this opposite of life. In effect, he has opted for a non-spiritual force whose existence is only transient and which ultimately ceases to live. Thus the sinner enters the realm known as death. The sin is anti-God and thus anti-life, and death — the ultimate anti-life — is the natural and inevitable by-product of sin.

Similarly, Adam's banishment from the Garden is more than a punishment. By the very nature of things, he can no longer remain in the Garden, because the Garden cannot contain a tarnished soul that has broken the law of God. That soul has now become infected with impurity, with desire, with temptation, with things of the flesh and not of the spirit. That soul, which has now introduced death into its very being, no longer has a place in God's eternal Garden.

V. *What is this that you have done?* Eve and Adam did something very fateful, with ramifications that affected all of mankind forever. Before the sin, Adam was almost a partner with God, as the verse states: *Hen ha-adam haya k'achad mimenu* (Genesis 3:22). As the Midrash relates it, Adam was a quasi-divine creature, and God escorts him through the Garden and shows him all its beauty, and informs him that all this has been created only for Adam's own pleasure and delight. God's own heavenly host attends to him, and God admonishes him: "Do not destroy my world" (*Kohelet Rabbah* 7; *Sanhedrin* 59b). But after the sin, all this is lost, and instead of living forever, as was God's original design, Adam invites death into the world for himself and his offspring forever, and he is banished from the Garden.

Now look at you: *Meh asita* indeed!

Excursus: The word asita has its root in the word aso, normally translated as "do" or "doing." But it is a term rich with meaning and numerous overlays. A breakdown of its use demonstrates that it means more than simply "do."

We find this term used frequently — though not universally — in reference to acts that are not looked upon with favor, that have negative consequences. In addition to the examples quoted above, the following citations offer further evidence of aso as referring to actions that are looked upon with disfavor. For this reason, the word "perpetrate," with its negative overtones, may occasionally be a more accurate translation for aso than the neutral word "do."

▸ *God says to the serpent ki asita zot — "because you have done this ...." (Genesis 3:14)*

▸ *Avimelekh to Abraham, when Avimelekh discovers that Sarah is really Abraham's wife: Mah asita — "What have you done," and mah ra-ita ki asita — "what did you see that [caused you] to do this? (ibid. 20:9)*

▸ *Jacob to Laban, after being cheated by him: Mah zot asita — "What is this that you have done?" (ibid. 29:25)*

- *Laban accusing Jacob of lying to him and of kidnapping his daughters: Meh asita* — "What have you done?" (ibid. 31:26)

- *Dinah's brothers, after their assault on Shechem: Hakezonah yaaseh et achoteinu* — "Shall our sister be done [made] as a harlot?" (ibid. 34:31).

- *The brothers of Joseph, upon discovering the planted goblet in Benjamin's knapsack: Mah zot asa Elo-him lanu* — "What is this that God has done to us?" (ibid. 42:28).

- *Joseph the Viceroy to his brothers: Mah hamaaseh hazeh asher asitem* — "What is this deed that you have done?" (ibid. 44:15)

- *Joseph's messenger, to the brothers, accusing them of theft: Hareiosem asher asitem* — "You have done evil in what you have done." *The brothers, in response to the accusation: Chalilah me-asot kadova ha-zeh* — It would be unseemly for us do such a thing" (ibid. 44:57).

- *God decides not to destroy Israel after the sin of the Golden Calf: Vayinachem haShem al hara-'ah asher diber laasot l'amo* — "And God repented Himself from the evil which He had thought to do to His people" (ibid. 32:14).

- *The Israelites complaining to Moses: Mah zot asita lanu* — "What is this that you have done to us?" (ibid. 14:11).

- *Moses says to his brother Aaron after the sin of the Golden Calf: Meh asah lecha haam haazeh* — "What has this people done to you?" (ibid. 32:21).

- *King Saul asks his son Jonathan about his drinking of the honey despite Saul's orders for a general fast: Mah asita?* — "What have you done?" (I Samuel 14:43).

- *Jeremiah, decrying the idolatrous ways of Israel: Meh asit?* (Jeremiah 2:23).

4

*... And it happened when they were in the field,
that Cain rose up against his brother Abel and
slew him. The Lord said to Cain: Where is Abel
your brother? And he said, I do not know. Am I
my brother's keeper?*

Genesis 4:8-10

MAN'S FIRST QUESTION TO GOD:
AM I MY BROTHER'S KEEPER?

The very first dialogue between God and man begins with
God's question to Adam: "Where are you?" (Genesis 3:9). The dialogue between God and Adam's son, Cain, also begins with a
question: "Where is Abel your brother?" (ibid. 4:9).

Adam does not respond to his question. Instead, he explains
that he is hiding because he is fearful. Cain does not hide. He
responds to God's question with his own question — the very first
question of man to God: *Hashomer achi anochi?* — "Am I my
brother's keeper?" (ibid. 4:9).

This is not a question conceived in wonder and innocence, in
which Cain explains that he was unaware that he was to be the
protector of his brother, that no one had informed him that this
was his responsibility. This is a question conceived in insolence
and defiance. For note the variations in man's reply to God's

question: Adam when confronted, answers directly, "I feared, so I hid." Then he proceeds to blame it on Eve. And Eve when asked blames it on the serpent. Though neither will accept the blame, clearly each of them feels some contrition. But Cain, when asked, feels no guilt: "Am I my brother's keeper?" *Why do you ask me where my brother is? Am I then the Creator, the Protector? It is not my duty but Yours to protect him, to keep him in life. If he is now dead, it not my doing, but Yours, Whose task it is to watch over all Your creatures. You failed to protect him, so he is dead. It is not I who am my brother's keeper; it is You.*

The disdain and arrogance are palpable. *When was I assigned to be my brother's keeper? If You want him, find him Yourself! What have I to do with my brother?* This is not a question at all. It is a retort at once impudent and sneering.

Note that Cain's retort consists of three crucial words; *keeper, brother,* and *I*.

Keeper: Shomer. The word is first encountered at the beginning of the Torah, where Adam and Eve are commanded to live in the Garden, to work it, and *leshamrah*, to keep it and protect it. The term is found later in the second set of Ten Commandments:

Shamor et Yom HaShabbat — "Keep (protect) the Shabbat day" (Deuteronomy 5:12).

Brother: That which should be a natural relationship of love and caring has a tortuous history in the Torah: Cain kills his brother Abel; Ishmael is the rival of his brother Isaac; Esau hates his brother Jacob; the brothers are envious of Joseph. (The genuine love between Moses and his brother Aaron is an exception to this rule of fraternal conflict.)

I: The Hebrew word *anochi* is the first word of the Ten Commandments, the pronoun by which God refers to His very Self: "I am the Lord your God ..." There can be only one *Anochi* in the universe. But man is to emulate the one *Anochi*; he is to become the kind of "I" who protects and keeps and cares.

Keeper, Brother, I. These represent the three elements which comprise every individual:

The being of the person, the *I.*

The reaching out to the non-I who is the brother of the *I.*

And the manifestation of this reaching out by being a *shomer* who shares, cares, protects, and loves.

These are three constants that must exist in every human being, in a delicate balance one with the other.

But in Cain they are not in balance. He affirms only the I; he denies the idea of Brother, and scoffs at the idea of Keeper.

Many years later, God will issue a bedrock commandment to the Children of Israel, and it will become known as the *k'lal gadol,* the Great Principle of the Torah (*Yerushalmi Nedarim* 9:4).

It will also contain three words: *Veahavta l're'acha kamocha* "Love thy neighbor as thyself" (Leviticus 19:18). Cain's impudent retort to God turns the three crucial words — Love, Neighbor, Self — on their face.

To *love* is to *keep, protect.*

Thy neighbor is your *brother.*

As *thyself* is the "I."

Cain anticipates the great commandment of the Lord, and he tramples on it even before it is uttered. For Cain there is no love, no neighbor, no brother. There is only self.

This is the source of Cain's insolence; it is begotten in selfishness. It is a gauntlet thrown at the Creator, a statement that claims that man is responsible only for himself and for no one else, that only he exists in this world.

Cain is the quintessential today-man, the this-world man, the creature of the now. For him tomorrow does not exist, for him there is no world-to-come. He is *oved ha-adamah,* the tiller of the earth, the physical, the material. Matters of heaven and of the spirit — these are fanciful, useless notions which bring no gratification to the senses.

Cain is an instinctive man, he who acts only in the interests of his self. He kills when his instinct tells him to, and then rejects all responsibility for his actions. He requires only one justification: Is it good for me? Does it give me pleasure? He lives to do as he pleases.

Thus it is no wonder that when Cain brings an offering to the Lord, it is something of little worth. It is "of the fruit of the ground" (Genesis 4:3), a very ordinary offering, whereas his brother Abel sacrifices the "firstlings of his flock and from their choicest" (*ibid.* 4:4), a special, valuable offering.

But man is not an animal created to behave by instinct and whose primary purpose is to serve the self. Man's task is to overcome the merely animal, the merely instinctive within him.

This is the purpose of the Torah: to help elevate us onto a new plateau in which we are able to do that which is not instinctive and natural; more, to transform the unnatural into the natural. The natural instinct is to be my own keeper; through the Torah, the unnatural instinct — to become the concerned, caring, willing keeper of my brother — becomes the natural.

Cain's insolent question appears in the fourth chapter of the Torah. The balance of the Torah — some one hundred and eighty-five more chapters — is an effort to teach man that the answer to this first question he asks of God is:

Yes, you are in fact your brother's keeper, for you and he are both creatures of Mine; you were both created by Me.
You are your brother's keeper:
You must assist him when he is downtrodden,
lend him what he needs,
help him with his heavy burdens,
leave the corner of your field for him if he is poor,
love him as you love yourself.
You are not alone in this world.
You are the keeper of your brother.
I created you and I created him,
and millions of others like you and like him.
You are all in My image,
and as I give you life,

and help you,
and give to you,
and support you,
so must you help and give and support one another.

He who rejects this brotherhood, who denies his one-ness with the other, becomes like a beast, diminished in his humanity and reduced to nothingness. Only he who has so diminished himself can bray insolently at his Creator and say:

I am not responsible for the care of my brother; You are. And since he has been killed, it is You who have failed him, not I. Am I then my brother's keeper? If You seek my brother, go find him.

God's very first question — to His creature Adam: "Where are you?"

God's subsequent question — to the son of Adam: "Where is Abel your brother?"

The two questions are not disconnected. Just as man and his self are not disconnected, so man and his brother are not disconnected: they are one. If a man knows where he himself is, he will know where his brother is. And if he knows where his brother is, he will know where he himself is.

And we, do we hear the questions addressed to us?

Do we know where we are?
Do we know where our brother is?
Do we, like Adam, seek to hide? Do we, like Cain, deny, rebel, defy, and wonder why we should be responsible for our brother, why we should not live for today, within this world, without a thought of tomorrow?

Cain, where is your brother?

There are two responses.

The first: *Am I my brother's keeper?*

And the second: *My brother is right here, by my side, for I am my brother and my brother is I. I am my brother's keeper, just as he who is my brother is my keeper.*

5

The Lord said to Cain ... Cursed are you from the earth. You shall become a wanderer on earth ...
Genesis 4:9-12

THE BEGINNING OF REGRET: *IS MY SIN TOO GREAT TO BEAR?*

At the beginning of history, two prototypes are presented to us. Abel is a keeper of sheep, and his brother, Cain, is a tiller of the soil. Cain brings as an offering to God the fruit of the ground. Abel, too, brings an offering: the firstlings of his flock. God is pleased by Abel's offering, but is not pleased by the offering of Cain, apparently because Abel's offering represents the best of his possessions ("the firstborn and their fat"), while Cain's is more miserly ("from the fruit of the ground," but not from the *choice* fruit).

Cain is very angry.

"It came to pass, when they were in the field, that Cain rose up against his brother Abel and killed him" (Genesis 4:8).

God punishes Cain and tells him that he is cursed and that he will be a vagabond and fugitive on the earth. Cain, in verse 13, then makes a curious statement to God: *Gadol avoni mineso*. There are several ways to read this. It can be read as a indicative sentence in which Cain is saying, "My sin is too great to (bear)." Read this way, it is a statement expressing regret, remorse, contrition, and repentance. This is certainly a legitimate rendering of the Hebrew.

However, Rashi reads it as a question of Cain to God: "Is my sin too great [for You, O God] to forgive?" Rashi bases his rendering on *Talmud Sanhedrin* 101b and on *Midrash Rabbah,* and interprets the verse in this way:

> *Read it as a question: You, O God, bear the worlds above and below — yet is only my sin impossible for you to bear? (Rashi understands that the Hebrew word "neso" can be rendered either as "to bear" or "to forgive.")*

In the straight, declarative reading, Cain is the one who bears the burden of the sin. In the interrogative reading, it is God Who bears the burden of the sin.

There is another subtle difference between the two readings, however. If it is a simple statement of fact, it expresses remorse and regret: my sin is so great I cannot bear it. If, however, it is a question, the remorse seems somewhat incomplete. Yes, Cain admits that it was a sin, but he seems to challenge God and to wonder petulantly why God finds it so heinous a crime: "You bear all kinds of things in Your universe. You bear the entire universe of above and below. Why can You not also bear the burden of my sin?"

If this is the meaning of Cain's words, it cannot be read as a pure expression of regret. He does not seem to recognize the gravity of his deed. In the eternal scheme of things, he seems to be saying, it is not of great significance: Yes, I sinned, but why are You so upset by it, You Who are the Master of all things?

But perhaps we are being unfair to Cain. Much depends on the tone of voice. Maybe there is genuine contrition here: "Can You not forgive me, You Who already carry the entire universe? I beg of You to bear the additional burden of my sin and to forgive me." Or as *Sanhedrin* 101b puts it: "You will some day forgive the sins of hundreds of thousands of Israelites; can You not forgive my one sin?"

In either reading, we have here the Bible's first explicit manifestation of regret for one's sin. Adam and Eve also transgress the
command of God, but even after they are found out we hear only
explanations and rationalizations — and, although there are oral
traditions that they did repent, we do not find any expressions of
remorse in the Biblical text.

A brief but illuminating aside on the issue of remorse for sin:

Much later in the Bible, King Saul commits a major transgression which marks a turning point in his kingship and the end of his
favor in the eyes of God — a subject we will discuss in greater detail
below. King David also commits a major transgression — but this
does not mark the end of his kingodom. Why is Saul's reign
doomed, while David's is not?

Saul's transgression is reported in I Samuel, Chapter 15. He
had been commanded to destroy all of Amalek, including its King
Agag, but Saul does not do so. "Saul and the people took pity on
Agag, on the best of the sheep, the cattle and the fatted bulls, the
fatted sheep, and on all that was good, they did not destroy
them" (15:9).

For this violation, Samuel informs Saul that God has ended his
kingdom.

David's transgression involves Bat-Sheba, wife of Uriah the Hittite.

Because he wants Bat-Sheba for himself, David arranges for
her husband to be placed in the front line of battle where he will
be killed (see II Samuel 11:14). The prophet Nathan excoriates
David for his action (12:7 ff.). (Note that the Talmud (*Shabbat*
56a) states that David was not guilty of the cardinal trangression
of pursuing another man's wife, since Bat-Sheba had already
received a conditional divorce from Uriah; and that Uriah was
already liable for the death penalty because he was rebellious
against the king. [See also Tosafot ibid., s.v. *"likuchin"* and s.v
"d'amar"; *Sanhedrin* 107a; *Gittin* 73b; and *Yoma* 22b.] Also

illuminating are the commentaries of Abarbanel at I Kings 15:5, and of Malbim at our text in II Samuel. See also the Artscroll commentary, ibid.)

Contrast the reaction of the two kings to the accusatory fingers of their prophets. Saul rationalizes to Samuel that he fulfilled almost all of the command; then he blames the people, and explains that he was fearful of them. But he does not express any regret or contrition. Like Cain before him, he does not seem to recognize the gravity of his sin.

But when Nathan says to David, "You are that man" (II Samuel 12:7) who has taken advantage of Uriah in order to take his wife for himself, and continues to denounce David in very harsh terms, David immediately recognizes his sin, confesses, and expresses sincere remorse in two simple but powerful words:

David said unto Nathan: *Chatati laShem* "I have sinned against the Lord" (II Samuel 12:13).

That Saul's transgression results in the end of his kingship (I Samuel 15:11), while David's transgression results in personal punishment but not in the cessation of his kingship (II Samuel 12:15 ff.), can be directly traced to their respective reactions to their sins. King Saul does not immediately recognize his sin and does not engage in pure repentance; David's reaction is swift: he both recognizes and repents.

All of which brings us to the issues of sin and forgiveness.

What is sin? The act of sinning contains several elements. In its extreme manifestation, to sin is to rebel against God, to defy His authority. He has told me not to behave in a certain way, but despite His command I will do as I please. He will not control my life, he will not tell me how to live. This is expressed by the Hebrew word *pesha'*, as in the famous passage in Isaiah 1:2: "Children I have raised and exalted, but they have rebelled *(pash'u)* against me." *Pesha'* is also used often in the sense of treachery and betrayal.

There is another type of sin, an action against God's will that stems not from my rebellion against Him but from an overpowering temptation within me that I cannot resist. I do not wish to rebel against my Creator, I love him and fear Him, but I am unable to resist stealing this object, or slandering that person; I find it difficult not to violate this holy day; I cannot say *No* to that overpowering desire that I know is wrong. This is expressed by the Hebrew word *avon.*

There is yet a third kind of sin, one that is not deliberate at all, but unintentional. I was careless, I gave it no thought, I forgot, I did not know it was forbidden, I am a creature of habit and before I knew it I was in violation, say, of Yom Kippur. This is expressed by the Hebrew word *chet* or *chatat,* which has its root in the word meaning "to miss the mark." It refers to an inadvertent, careless veering off the path. It also suggests a disregard for God, because one who is fully aware of God's presence does not act out of instinct or habit. The truly religious person does not forget that God exists and that He commands.

When Moses pleads with God to forgive Israel for the sin of the Golden Calf, he describes God as the *nossei avon, va-pesha, v'chata-ah* (Exodus 34:7), who bears — or forgives — the three kinds of sin (perhaps suggesting that Israel was guilty of all three variations of sin in the Calf worship). In Numbers 13:18, after the rebellion of the spies, we read the same phrase, but "*chata-ah*" is omitted.

Cain describes his sin as *avon.* His act was not meant to defy God. He simply was overwhelmed by his instincts and in his anger he killed his brother. According to the Sages (see *Sanhedrin* 37b) he did not even know how to go about ending someone's life. (*Yoma* 36b discusses these three kinds of sin. Note also that there are other terms for sin, such as *aveirah,* which is an overall term for transgression, as used in Avot 3:1 and elsewhere. See also our chapter above which analyzes the nature of sin.)

In one form or another, to sin is to veer from the path that God has set out for us, to go off on our own, to turn our back on God and walk away from Him. And repentance — the Hebrew term is *teshuvah*, literally, "return" — is to return to the path, to turn the self around, to face God again instead of turning our back to Him, and to begin walking towards Him.

Each of us is familiar with sin, not only the sins of others but also our very own (though our own are rarely seen as clearly as those of others). Most of our sinning does not fall under the rubric of *pesha',* the deliberate rebellion against God's authority. Most of our sinning is of the garden variety: it is due to human weakness, or inability to withstand temptation, or carelessness, or rationalizing, or ignorance, or passion, anger, or jealousy. Even as we violate the commandments of God we continue to believe in Him, as witness the famous comment of the Sages about the thief who prays to God to help him just before he breaks into someone's house: *Ganva apum machtarta rachamana krei* — "The thief at the entrance to the tunnel [which he is digging to break into someone's house] calls on God to help him." (*Berachot* 63a, in Munich ms. cited in *Dikdukei Soferim* and *Ein Yaakov, Berachot* 63a, n. 40. See also Mossad HaRav Kook edition of *R. Bachya, Kad haKemach, Shaar Habitachon*, fn. 36.)

But even ordinary sinning moves us away from God. In order to be rectified and erased, any kind of sin — even a careless one — requires regret, contrition, and a turning back towards Him. This is not an easy task. It requires honest recognition, confession, and admission that one has done wrong. But if one is sincerely contrite and pledges to change his direction, the sin is wiped away. This is the meaning of *kippur* in Hebrew: a "wiping away."

The very concept of *teshuvah* and its promise of being granted full pardon by God and of returning to Him is a gift from Above. God could have decreed that the sinner be forever banished from His Presence; that for the one who violates the directives from God there is no path of return ("No U-Turn," as the highway signs tell us); that he must go through life as a permanent outcast from his Creator, never again to have any connection to Him. That God chooses instead to allow us to make that turnaround — that He in fact encourages it — indicates that repentance, forgiveness, and reconciliation are essential components of God's design for the universe, a signal that God knows our weaknesses, recognizes our failings, and is patient with our stubborness; and that He welcomes us with outstretched hand when we decide to turn back towards Him.

It also suggests something beyond this: that a sin creates an imperfection in God's plan for the world, and distorts His design for the universe. God's commandments are of two kinds: the positive thou-shalt's and the negative thou-shalt-not's. When one performs a thou-shalt, one shares in the building of the universe: one has added a building block to the Divine structure that God has planned. But when one sins — that is, violates a thou-shalt-not — one has destroyed a building block, or at the very least pulled a block out of place. Thus, a sin has a negative impact not only on the sinner, but also on the universe itself. Only regret and repentance can return that block to its rightful place, and restore God's design for the universe.

That is perhaps why the Hebrew word *neso* means both "to bear" and "to forgive." In the ordinary sense, when God forgives a sin, he "bears" it, endures it, and erases it. In a deeper sense, a sin moves the world off in a different direction, and God, who has given free will to man, must suffer with it, must bear it, must carry this burden. This, as we have seen, is the word Cain uses in his cry to God: *Gadol avoni mineso?* — "Is my sin too great to bear?" And this is the word Moses uses in describing God's goodness (Exodus 34:7): ... *nosse avon,* — "...bears (or forgives) sin." He who forgives does in fact agree to bear the burden of the sin and not to cast it back upon the shoulders of the sinner. (See also, among many other examples, Micah 7:18: "Who is a God like You, *nosse avon* — forgiving (or bearing) sin — *v'over al pesha'* — and forgiving transgression"; and Psalms 85:3: *nassata avon amecha* — "You have forgiven (or borne) the sin of Your people.")

This is Cain's cry to God: "Is my sin too great to bear?" I do not deny my sin. I have taken a life, and that is a major transgression against You, the Giver of Life. I confess my sin, and I regret it. But nothing is too heavy for the Creator of the universe to bear. I beg You to bear my sin as well, to forgive it and to allow me to live out my life.

In one form or another, each one of us sins. Most of our sinning is not of the rebellious variety, but of the can't-help-myself variety. We do not intend to challenge God's authority. We want only to satisfy our desires and temptations.

But all sinning upsets God's plans for the world, and the only way it can be set aright again is for us to address our failings, recognize them, confess them before God, and resolve not to repeat them. Sincere return, *teshuvah*, creates the miracle of wiping the sin away and — according to the Sages — of transforming the sin into a mitzvah.

Teshuvah is a powerful act, a wondrous gift from Above. But it is probably the most difficult act for a human being to initiate: to recognize that he is imperfect, that he erred, and to admit this to himself and to God (and to others whom he might have wronged).

Precisely because it is so difficult to do, are its rewards so staggering — for the Sages inform us that when someone repents sincerely out of love of God, his earlier sins are transformed into mitzvot.

Whether Cain engaged in sincere repentance ("My sin is too great to forgive") or only in a somewhat reluctant repentance ("Is my sin too great for You to forgive?") we do not know. But he clearly recognized that what he had done was an offense against God, and he made no attempt to rationalize, explain away, or deny his sin. It is ironic: Cain, the world's first murderer, he who commits one of the cardinal transgressions, is also the world's first penitent, expressing remorse, contrition, and a desire to return.

A question worth pondering: whose sin was greater, Cain's or that of his parents, Adam and Eve? Cain was never explicitly told not to kill anyone, though he surely knew that this was a transgression against God, since the fundamental norms — to be known as the Noachide Code — were already given to Adam. (*Sanhedrin* 56ff., esp. 59b; *Maimonides, Mishneh Torah, Hil. Melachim* 9:1) But he was never directly told not to kill. On the other hand, he actually snuffed out a life, which is a violation of a fundamental norm, and one of the cardinal sins. As for Adam and Eve, while they did sin, they did not kill anyone. They only ate of the fruit. But unlike Cain, the eating did willfully violate a direct and explicit command by God.

Further questions: If Adam and Eve had not violated God's command, would Cain have violated the command not to kill? Did the action of the parents make it possible for the son to break the law in his own way? The parents gave way to temptation; the son gave way to his anger.

If the parents had had the strength to resist temptation, would the son have had the strength to resist his anger?

6

And the men arose from there and looked toward Sodom. And Abraham went with them, to bring them on the way. And God said, "Shall I conceal from Abraham that which I intend to do?"

Genesis 18:16-17

GOD'S QUESTION TO HIMSELF: *SHALL I CONCEAL FROM ABRAHAM...?*

God asks Himself a question:

Hamechaseh Ani meAvraham asher Ani oseh — "Shall I conceal from Abraham that which I intend to do?" (lit., "that which I do?").

It is a straightforward question, open, colloquial, almost ingenuous in its simplicity — which makes it all the more striking when we bear in mind that the one asking the question is the One Himself.

The question is of course rhetorical. Its meaning is, *To conceal My plans from Abraham is clearly unthinkable.*

To an ordinary reader, however, the very question is unthinkable:
The Creator of the universe,
He who formed the blazing, life-giving sun
and the cold and distant moon;

He who is Master and Creator of the endless galaxies;
The Giver of all life,
the Author of all existence,
He Who is Omnipotent,
and Omnisicient,
and Omnipresent,
the Being and the Essence of the universe —
He asks Himself — as if it were a preposterous notion —
Shall I conceal My intentions from Abraham?

The question is beyond comprehension: Of course God can conceal His plans — from Abraham and from anyone else!

True, Abraham is the great revolutionary who brought God into the world of mankind. He is the personification of God's own *chesed*/lovingkindness, and he lives a life devoted to God and humanity. But he is only a mortal human being who, in his own words, is "dust and ashes," here today and tomorrow no longer. That God should ask such a question almost borders on the absurd.

✍ *Abraham's Uniqueness*

How is it that Abraham is someone with whom God feels he must consult?

The unique relationship beween Abraham and God is underscored in many contexts — particularly in matters of theodicy. The great Biblical figures were all concerned with the issue of why the righteous suffer and the wicked prosper. Moses, for example, begs God to reveal His essence to him, to explain His ways to him — *hodi'eini na et derachecha* (Exodus 33:13) and "show me Your Glory" — *hareini na et kevodecha* (ibid. 33:18) — which, according to the Sages, is a petition to understand the ultimate question of why the righteous suffer (cf. *Berachot* 7a, and *Yalkut Shim'oni* 395, at this verse). God replies that it is not within the capacity of mortal man to comprehend God's ways, "for no man can see Me and live" (Exodus 33:20). Granted, you are Moses, and in all My house you are the most trustworthy (ne-eman), and you are My greatest prophet, and you speak to Me "face to face as a man speaks to his friend" (ibid. 33:11). But despite your greatness and My profound love for you, says God, all I can reveal to you is achorai, My back, but not My face, not My essence. (See the final chapter in this volume for a fuller discussion of this theme.)

Thus is the petitition of Moses rejected. Admittedly, his request is extremely far reaching: a mortal man desires to comprehend the Immortal One. It is hardly surprising, and no derogation of Moses, that his petition is denied.

Look also at the very embodiment of suffering, the Biblical Job. God Himself describes him as "My servant Job, for there is no one like him on the earth, a man perfect and upright, who fears God and refrains from evil" (Job 1:8) — a description echoed by the Bible itself in the very first verse of that book. But when Job, after all of his calamities, wants to know why all this has befallen him, who has served God so faithfully, God replies from His whirlwind and asks almost tauntingly:

> Where were you when I laid the foundations of the earth ...?
> Who fixed her measurements ...?
> Who closed up the sea ...?
> Have you spread out the sky ...?

That section of Job (chapter 36 ff.) is an awesome account of the power of God, but what Job learns from it is essentially what Moses learned from God's reply to his own question: you are a finite being and I am Infinite; you are a mortal man, limited in your capacity to perceive the eternal and the Eternal One — your mind cannot possibly contain God's truths and God's reasons and God's ways. In effect, Moses and Job are informed that, as Isaiah 55:8 phrases it, "My thoughts are not your thoughts, nor are your ways My ways ...."

But note God's reaction when Abraham raises the same question. In Genesis 15 he intercedes on behalf of the people of Sodom, and he says to God that it is not just or right that the good people who might be in Sodom should perish together with the wicked. "Will the Judge of the earth not do righteousness?" (ibid. 15:25).

Although Abraham here also touches on the very essence of God's conduct of the world, God does not instruct him, as he will later instruct Moses in Exodus 33, to climb into the cleft of the rock to view God's back; God does not mysteriously show Abraham the back of His "head" but not His "face" because God's face — His essence — cannot be seen. And God does not challenge Abraham, as He does Job, for his apparent effrontery by asking him if he knows how to create stars or planets or oceans or mountain ranges. Instead, God engages Abraham in a most gentle negotiation. (See our Chapter 7 for further discussion of this negotiation.)

Apparently, Abraham may say things to his Creator that no one else may say. He is like the valued confidant of the king who can do anything and say anything even in the very throne room, and who can vex and hector the king in ways that, were he a commoner, would call for a beheading. Abraham can challenge the manner in which the Creator governs His world as no one else can challenge it — not even His loyal servant Moses, not even His loyal servant Job. The Midrash recognizes this when it states that although Abraham and Job each confronted God about His apparent injustice, "Abraham received a reward for this, and Job was punished for this." (*Bereshit Rabbah* 49:9) It is no wonder that Isaiah 41:8 refers to him as "Abraham My beloved" (*Avraham ohavi*), and that II Chronicles 20:7 refers to him as "Abraham Your beloved" (*Avraham ohavcha*). Similarly, in *Pirke d'R. Eliezer* 25 — cited in Rashi at Genesis 18:17 — Abraham is once again *ohavi* — "My beloved."

Yalkut Shim'oni 927 on Job offers the following poignant insight, based on God's cryptic statement in Job 41:4: "I will not be silent with him .... (*lo acharish badav*)."

Said the Holy One, Blessed is He: "Mankind should not say, We will also speak before the Lord as Abraham did, and He will be silent before us" (v'hu shotek lanu). Said the Holy One, Blessed is He: "I will not be silent with him [Job]" — "I was silent only with Abraham, for he was silent before Me: I had said to him, 'For in Isaac shall your seed be called' (Genesis 21:12), and then I said to him, 'Take your son [Isaac] for a sacrifice' — and he was silent before Me. Therefore I will also be silent before him (af Ani acharish lo), even though he spoke harsh words (devarim kashim).... [as in ibid. 18:23] And Abraham said, "Will You destroy the righteous with the wicked?" Said Abraham: "So that the idolaters shall not say, 'This is God's practice, to destroy various generations cruelly: the generation of Enosh, the generation of the Flood, the generation of the Dispersion (dor hapalagah)' ...."

Abraham is the beloved one of the king/King who is informed of his/His actions in advance. To be sure, God regularly reveals His intentions to His prophets — this, after all, is what prophecy is all about — but nowhere does He declare that it would be unthinkable not to reveal them. Only in this instance is God so explicit.

A brief excursus: Although it takes us far afield, it is noteworthy that throughout the classic texts we find curious connecting links between Abraham and Job. For example, the identical word is used to describe each of them: Abraham is told to circumcise himself and become "tamim/perfect/whole," and Job in the very first verse is described as "tam." (Noah and Jacob are so described as well.) When Satan appears before God at the beginning of the book of Job, the Rabbinic tradition has it that Satan compares Job to Abraham (Rashi at Job 1:7). Satan, never resting, also appears to Abraham on the way to the akeida and attempts to dissuade him from fulfilling God's command (Sanhedrin 89b). Note also Avot d'R. Nassan 7:1, which recounts God's rebuke of Job: while you are a good man, *you are not like Abraham who built a palace to help wayfarers and prepared food and drink for them, whereas you, Job, although righteous, remained at home. That is to say, Abraham was righteous actively, while Job was righteous passively. It is also important to note, in connection with their respective disquisitions with God about Divine justice, a significant difference between the two. When Job challenges God it is because of his personal suffering. When Abraham challenges God, it is not for himself but for the residents of Sodom, a people he does not even know. Further, when God commands him to sacrifice his own son Isaac — which on the surface is an obvious contradiction of all of God's promises to him about his future and the future people Israel — Abraham does not question God about His justice. And while Moses does intervene for others, his intervention is not for a strange and unknown people, but for his own followers, the children of Israel. [For a thorough analysis of the connections between Abraham and Job, see the perceptive ArtScroll Iyov/Job commentary by R. Moshe Eisemann, p. 370.*

✍ The Beloved One

Abraham has become so one-dimensional in our eyes — he was the first Jew, he broke the idols, he brought monotheism to the world, he was willing to sacrifice everything for God — that we tend to overlook the essence of this man whose bond with God is so close and so secure. What is the special quality unique to Abraham that makes him the beloved one of God?

This is a question not easily addressed. When it comes to understanding the reasons for God's behavior, we can only blend together a mixture of speculation, guesswork, and conjecture, stir carefully, and pray that some reasonably palatable brew will emerge.

The essential Abraham emerges when he is placed side by side with Moses. Here we have two seminal figures of the Bible. The one is the great revolutionary, who, as the precursor of the people Israel, brings God into the world; the other is the great prophet and leader who with his very life shapes and forms the people Israel. They stand as twin colossi at the entrance to Judaism. Without either of them, there would be no Jewish people, no Torah, no Land of Israel, no bearers of God's word in His universe. Who would be presumptuous enough even to whisper that God's bond to the one is stronger than His bond to the other?

Nevertheless, certain matters do stand out. Abraham, for example, has one major advantage over Moses in their respective relationships to God. Moses is the great teacher — *Moshe Rabbenu* — who teaches all men how to live the godly life. And he is, of course, the greatest of all the prophets, speaking to God "as a man speaks to his friend" (Exodus 33:11). The climactic verses at the end of the Torah stand as God's eternal tribute to him: "There arose no other prophet in Israel like Moses, whom God knew face to face" (Deuteronomy 34:10).

And yet, despite all this, it cannot be denied that it is Abraham and not Moses who is the first to bring God into this world. He is, in a way, the discoverer of God (*Bereshit Rabbah* 39:1; 64:4). *Midrash Tehillim* on Psalm 110 says it this way:

> The nations of the world slumbered and did not come under the wings of the Divine Presence. Who aroused them so they could rest under His wings? Abraham .... Not only did Abraham arouse the nations. The quality of righteousness also slumbered until Abraham aroused it. How? He built an inn that was open on all sides to welcome all wayfarers, invited them to his table, provided them with food, drink, and lodging [and taught them that there was only one Creator] ....

This is echoed in *Berachot* 7b: "From the day that the Holy One, Blessed is He, created the world, there was no man who called Him *Adon* ("Master") until Abraham came and called Him *Adon*, as in Genesis 15:8." Maimonides, in his *Laws of Idolatry*, I, describes vividly how Abraham travels throughout the ancient world in order to spread this teaching (Cf. *Sotah*

10a-b). Since Abraham in effect was engaged in converting mankind to the belief in the one God, he is to this very day known as the father of all proselytes, so that when a fresh convert to Judaism is given a Hebrew name, he is, regardless of his new given name, always *ben Avraham Avinu,* — "the son of Abraham our Father."

Abraham's connection with God is even deeper. So symbiotic with God's vision was Abraham, so congruent with His ways, that he anticipated and observed all the commandments of the Torah even before they were given at Sinai. (See final Mishnah in *Kiddushin*, and *Yoma* 28b.) There is nothing esoteric in this concept. Each individual commandment contains within it the kernel of some profound and mysterious truth about God and man. Abraham's soul was so identified with his Creator that he was able to apprehend on his own the eternal truths embedded in God's mitzvot. That is to say, his essence was in perfect harmony with God's essence. (See R. Menahem HaMeiri (Provence, 1249–1336), *Introduction to Avot* for a somewhat different perspective.)

It is true that God is the Master and Abraham the servant; true that God created Abraham and that Abraham is subservient to Him. But it might be said that just as God brought Abraham into being, so also, in a manner of speaking, did Abraham bring God into being — in this world. For many years prior to Abraham, there was no knowledge of God on earth. It was Abraham who brought this knowledge and this awareness of God's singular existence into the consciousness of mankind. Obviously, God the Eternal One exists independently of Abraham, but without Abraham, He would be a God without a mankind to worship Him, a Creator Whom mankind does not recognize or know. As R. Bachya ben Asher (13th century) states pithily in his *Kad Hakemach* (chapter on Rosh Hashanah), *Ein melech b'lo am* — "One cannot be a king without a people." Only through Abraham does God — the God Who is One and Who is Alone — begin to exist for all mankind. Abraham is the pioneer of God, the trailblazer.

This concept of discovering God should not descend into clichés. Through this discovery, Abraham initiates the process of the redemption of mankind. For the purpose of the Torah and of God's Presence in history is to create a connecting bridge between man and God. By bringing God into the world, Abraham constructs the all-important first plank in this bridge. It is only after that first plank is firmly set down that others can come along to complete the structure. And when the Messiah finally appears to redeem the people Israel and mankind, that will mark the completion of the bridge that had its beginning in Abraham.

A brief but tantalizing excursus: Paradoxically, the Messiah traces his origins back to Sodom. The Messiah is from the lineage of King David, and King David's great-great-grandmother is Ruth (Ruth 4:21-22). Ruth is from the land of Moab, and the original Moab's mother is none other than the daughter of Lot, nephew of Abraham. After fleeing the destruction of Sodom, she gives birth, by her father's seed, to Moab (Genesis 19:30-37). The plans that God will not conceal from Abraham are the plans for the destruction of Sodom. It is tempting to flesh out the Messianic chiaroscuro of this entire episode, but that exploration must be left for another time. Suffice it to say that Abraham's presence is manifest both at the beginning of mankind's redemption and at the Messianic climax of that redemption.

As a sign of this man-God connection, Abraham is given the *berit*, the covenant of circumcision — which represents the utilization of the physical in service of the spiritual and thus symbolizes the connection between man, the material one, and God, the spiritual One. As the first to fulfill God's *berit* covenant on his own physical self, Abraham once again becomes the initiator: he takes the first step in the human journey to connect earth and heaven.

The commentary of Malbim (R. Meir Malbim, Eastern Europe, 1809–1879) on God's question to Himself touches on Abraham's role as pioneer:

> .... Abraham became the conduit (tzinor) through which Divine Providence (hashgachah) came down to the earth. Were it not for Abraham ... the affairs of the world would have been given over [not to God's Providence] but to the quirks of nature. Abraham brought God's Providence to the world, because he was the first [emphasis added] to bring His Presence (Shechinah) down to the earth ....

Perhaps this is why the connection between God and Abraham is so extraordinary. When God states that it is quite natural to keep Abraham informed, He is expressing the profound affection that the Immortal One feels towards this mortal, finite human being who had the perception and the courage to bring the Infinite into the world, to introduce Him to humanity, and to begin the process of the redemption of mankind.

Does God need man's awareness? Yes. Although God is Alone in His separateness and uniqueness — which is the real meaning of God as Echad/One — He nevertheless desires to be known in the universe. For the core of God is His goodness. As He tells Moses when He is about to reveal certain aspects of Himself to him, "I will cause all My goodness to pass before you ...." (Exodus 33:19; cf also Jeremiah 31:13; Psalms 31:20). The constituent element of goodness is that it cannot remain isolated; it must by definition reach out and share itself with others. But if no others are aware of God, this goodness cannot touch them or reach them. Only through an acknowledgment of God's Presence in the universe — only by being an integral part of the affairs of man — can God's goodness be made manifest in this world. When this occurs, man has the possibility of achieving what his soul most desires: the spiritual joy and inner harmony that come from an intimate connection with the Creator.

But if man is unaware of God's Presence, His goodness remains, as it were, contained, bottled up, and restricted to the heavenly spheres, unable to radiate outward. God's goodness can enter the world only when man is conscious of His Presence. Since Adam, God had been waiting, so to speak, for the one man to appear who can bring man to God, and God to man, so the bridge between them can be constructed. Of all the great men who enter the stage of history after Adam — Enoch, Noah, Shem, Ever — no one possesses the perfection of character and the ideal symbiosis of body and soul to effect this revolution. Until Abraham appears. Only he has the spiritual power to release God's holiness and goodness from its heavenly confines and enable it to flow freely throughout the world (Cf. *Midrash Rabbah* Genesis 49:2).

God acknowledges Abraham, as it were, for bringing Him into the world. This acknowledgment, according to some of the Sages, is expressed in Psalms 110:1: "God says to my master (*la-adoni*), 'Wait at my right hand ....'" In a striking comment based on the Sages, Rashi writes that "my master" refers to none other than Abraham: "God says to Abraham, whom the nations called *adoni,* as [when the children of Het spoke to Abraham] in Genesis 23:5, [saying] 'Hear us, my master.'" That the Master Himself should even obliquely refer to Abraham as *adon*/master, would hardly be whisperable had not the Sages and Rashi offered this interpretation. In effect, just as there is one Master/*Adon* in heaven, there is one earthly master/*adon* in this world, and he is Abraham. This stunning Divine deference toward him surfaces again in *Midrash Rabbah* 39:17 (at Genesis 12:2) where God allows Abraham's name to precede His own in the *amidah,* and it is echoed when God Himself grants Abraham His ultimate imprimatur: "I am the Singular One (*Yechidi*) of My world, and Abraham is the singular one of his world ...." (*Pesachim* 118a). (See also Genesis 33:20; "Jacob erected an altar there, *vayikra lo* — and he called it — *El Elohe Yisrael.*" While the normative reading is that Jacob called the altar by this name, one Talmudic opinion (*Megillah* 18a, cited by Rashi; and *Midrash Rabbah* 79:9) suggests that the reading is: "And He [God] called him [Jacob] *el*" — which is another name for the Omnipotent One. However, in a variant reading, in this same Midrash, Jacob says to God, "You are the Lord of the higher spheres, and I am lord of the lower spheres." For this presumption of grandeur, says the Midrash, Jacob is punished by the abduction of his daughter Dinah, whose story begins in the very next verse of the Bible. The differing ascriptions of greatness to God and to Jacob engender much discussion among the commentators. Nahmanides warns that the matter is a *sod gadol* — a "profound mystery.")

ᕱᕰ *Of the Other Side*

Abraham is not only the trailblazer to God; he is also the first to be willing to surrender his own future and his own beliefs for the sake of God. For this is what the *akeida* represents: when Abraham obeys God's command to offer up his beloved son Isaac as a sacrifice, it is not only his son that he is willing to surrender: he also places on the altar his own future, as embodied in his son, plus the promise of the God Whom he trusts and Who had promised him that in "Isaac will your seed be called" — *ki b'Yitzchak yikare lecha zara* (Genesis 21:12) and Who, in *Genesis* 12:7, and again in 15:18, and again in 17:19, had promised Abraham "that the Land will be given to his seed" — *lezar'acha etein et ha-aretz hazot,* and Who in 17:21 had assured him that He would establish His covenant with Isaac. But Abraham is willing to sacrifice everything — not only his son but everything that this son represents for the future — for the sake of his unflinching obedience to God. Despite what appears to be the sundering of God's promise, Abraham, paradoxically, maintains his trust in that promise.

In this, he is similar, once again, to Job, who declares, "Though He slay me, I will still trust in Him (Job 13:15). It was Abraham, however, who created the prototype. There were many others in Jewish history who sacrificed their all for the sake of God. But Abraham was the first. In this context, "first" is not only a chronological term, but a spiritual one. It was he who branded within the collective Jewish soul the permanent imprint of sacrifice for God. When the famous Hannah (*Gittin* 57b in *II Maccabees,* 7) surrenders her seven sons rather than permit them to bow before an idol, she was enabled to do this by Abraham, who was prepared to offer his own sacrifice long before she did. The long line of Jewish martyrs owes its inner steel to the paradigm established by Abraham. As R. Chaim of Volozhin (1749–1821) suggests in his *Ruach Chaim* commentary at Avot 5:4, the unflagging Jewish love for the Land of Israel originates in Abraham's submission to God's call to abandon everything and to depart for that special Land, and the enduring Jewish capacity for religious martyrdom stems from his willingness to offer up his son at the *akeida.*

Similarly, there were many who came later who fought against the prevailing winds, and who stubbornly maintained their special relationship to God despite the enticements of the cultures around them. But it was Abraham who pioneered the way, and who made it possible for those who came later to live as heroic Jews. That is why it is said only of Abraham that he "came from the other side" — *Avraham ha-ivri* (Genesis 14:13). From the other side of the river not only geographically, but also spiritually: the entire world was on one side of the divide, and he alone was on the other. Abraham was the exemplar, and thus he became the beloved one of God.

There is more to the uniqueness of Abraham. Unlike all the Biblical figures who came after him, Abraham's father was an idolater, so that Abraham not only had to reject his social background to become a Jew, but also his familial one. He is the original iconoclast: one who breaks icons. When, in Genesis 12, God instructs Abraham, *Lech Lecha*, "Go from your land, from your birthplace, and from your father's house …." this is what is meant: you must leave everything behind you, including your own family, and strike out for the uncharted destination which I will show you. This, says *Yalkut Shim'oni* at Job 14:4: — "Who can make a clean thing out of an unclean thing, only One" — the "clean thing" refers to Abraham [who issued forth] from [his idolatrous father] Terach …."

Of all the great servants of God, no one else carries out the major rupture with his past that Abraham does in order to serve his Maker. In addition, no one who follows him has to endure the other trials and tests — the "ten trials" — that Abraham successfully undergoes (Avot 5:3).

Here we are given a glimpse into the meaning of the prophet in Amos 3:7: "The Lord will do nothing without revealing His secrets to His servants, the prophets." (Abraham is not only God's servant; in Genesis 20:7, he is also referred to as a prophet.) This is similar to David's declaration in Psalms 25:14: "The secret of the Lord is with them that fear Him" — an affirmation shared by David's son Solomon in Proverbs 3:32: "... [God shares] His secret (sodo) with the upright."

From all this there emerges an intriguing thought:
Abraham, the discoverer of God,
His beloved and His advocate,
the courageous destroyer of the anti-God idols,
the first to be in total harmony with God's ways ;
he who is from the other side and against the pagan world,
he who alone represents the God Who is alone,
who is God's conduit to mankind,
who initiates the bridge between the physical and the spiritual,
who surrenders everything to follow God to destinations unknown;
he who imprints this quality upon the Jewish soul forever,
he who is singular in this world as God is singular in His abode,
and who is the spiritual father of all believers in the One God —
— is it at all improbable to suggest that this Abraham has more than a special relationship with God, and that he is, in a spiritual sense, an associate of God, a partner with Him? So does he apparently view their relationship — negotiating with God as if he were a full-fledged member of the Divine court. And apparently God does not disagree. In fact, God uses a term about Abraham that connotes profound closeness: "For I have known him .... (ki yedativ)" (Genesis 18:19), which Rashi terms lashon chiba — "a term of

affection." The term *da'at*, "knowledge," is used to describe only the most intimate of relationships. (The same term is used in reference to Moses in Deuteronomy 34:10 — "... whom God has known (*asher yeda'o*) face to face.") And note the remarkable comment of the *Midrash Yalkut Shim'oni* 869 at Psalms 110:1 — "The Lord says to my master, 'Sit at my right hand ....' — At the end of days, the Holy One, Blessed is He, will seat the Messianic king at His right, and Abraham at His left ...."

"*Shall I conceal from Abraham that which I intend to do?*" Of course not. Partners and associates do not withhold information from one another.

✒ God's Partner

A word about that term, "partner with God." While it is not infrequent in Rabbinic literature, the connotation of "as if partner with the Holy One in the original Creation" (*k'ilu shutaf shel Hakadosh Baruch Hu b'ma'aseh bereishit*) — its connotation is not quite as sublime as that outlined above. It is used, rather, as an honorific granted to those who maintain the fundamental *grund-norms* of godliness and adhere to the principles of truth, self-control, and constant faith in God as the Creator. Thus, the following are called "partners in God's Creation":

▸ "*Whosoever issues a judgment according to its truth (hadan din emet l'amito) ....*" (*Shabbat* 10a);

▸ "*Whosoever hears a curse against himself and is silent although he has the possibility of protesting ....*" (*Midrash Tehillim* at Psalms 86);

▸ "*Whosoever prays on the eve of Shabbat and recites vayechulu....* (Genesis 2:1-3)

▸ "*The sixth day, and the heavens and the earth and all their hosts were completed*" (*Midrash Sechel Tov* at Exodus 16).

These are all partners in the Creation in that their deeds help actualize God's design for His world.

But these are symbolic titles, a series of "as if's." An individual who recites the proper prayer on Friday night is certainly not on the same level of partnership as is Abraham. To very few is vouchsafed the role of actual associate of God in His ongoing direction of His universe. Such a role is reserved only for the towering Biblical figures.

These figures all behave like concerned partners in a great enterprise. They all have an interest in the success of the enterprise and want to make certain that God's program, so to speak, should succeed. They want His reputation to spread. They do not want mankind to think ill of Him. Like true partners and associates, they are at home in the precincts of the Almighty. They speak openly with Him, never hesitating to question God whenever they feel that His Name will be diminished if certain actions are carried out.

Thus the Talmud in *Berachot* 31b lists various Biblical personalities who "spoke with audacity before heaven (*hitiach devarim kelapei maalah,* lit., "hurled words toward heaven"): Hannah, mother of the prophet Samuel; Elijah; and Moses. Elaborating on the audacity of Moses, *Berachot* 32a offers the remarkable image of Moses grasping the garment of God and not letting go:

> God says to Moses, "Now therefore let Me alone ...."
> (Exodus 32:10). Were it not explicitly written, it would not
> be possible to say such a thing: this teaches that Moses
> grasped the Holy One, Blessed Is He, like a man who seizes
> his friend by his garment, and said before Him: Sovereign
> of the universe, I will not let You go until You forgive and
> pardon [Israel].

The clear implication is that as long as Moses is very insistent, God will not act against his wishes, which is why God says, *hanicha li* — "let Me alone ...." That is, until you let Me alone, until you release Me, I cannot do what I wish to do as long as you object to it. Moses is thus a true partner with God. (God's unwillingness to act against the strong objections of Moses also beggars the imagination.

This Divine "Let Me alone" is the declarative counterpart of God's interrogative, "Shall I conceal ...." and deserves an essay of its own.)

And when the Torah describes the prayer of Moses on behalf of Israel, *"Vayechal Moshe" (Exodus 32:11)*, the Sages say that Moses exclaims," It is a profanation (*chulin*) of God's reputation and Holy Name to do such a thing, to destroy Israel" (*Berachot* 32a). (Abraham uses the same term in his dialogue with God about Sodom in Genesis 18:25: *chalila lecha*.) Moses is concerned with God's reputation in the wider world. *Lama yom'ru Mitzraim ...* — "Why should Egypt say, 'He brought them out to slay them in the mountains ...'" (Exodus 32:12). According to *Berachot* 32a, Moses says, "Now the nations of the world will say, 'God has grown feeble and is not able to deliver'" — a theme echoed, among other places, in Psalms 115:2: *Lama yom'ru haGoyim ayeh na Eloheihem* — "Why should the nations say, 'Where is their [Israel's] God?'" In the same Talmudic text, God responds with gratitude to Moses: "You have revived Me (i.e., preserved My estimation in the world) with your words."

Now, if the sense of partnership with God is not limited to Abraham, why is it especially toward Abraham that God seems to direct His intensified sense of affection, and why is he the only one among these exalted Biblical figures to whom the Creator feels obligated to confide His future intentions? Indeed, why not Moses?

Perhaps a hint of an answer lies in the concept adumbrated above: Abraham is the trailblazer. By definition, only one person can be the trailblazer and pioneer who establishes the paradigm for all of history. As profound as was the Divine connection with those who followed, only one person can be the first and the prototype of all that follows. That person becomes the beloved confidant of the Almighty One.

✺ Limitless Possibilities

After all is said and done, the questions raised here about God's question to Himself can have no definitive resolution, for no one can enter the mind of God. We mortals, we who are not partners and who have not created anything, much less whirlwinds, can only conjecture. We can only ask the questions and pray that in the fullness of time some approach to an answer will be vouchsafed us.

One insight, however, emerges unambiguously: quite beyond the issue of why Abraham is the beloved one, God's incredible question stands as a striking reminder of the limitless possibilities for human closeness and attachment to God. Man, who is but dust and ashes, who is frail and vulnerable and subject to the thousand ills of the flesh" bears within himself the Divine power — if he chooses to exercise this power by intense prayer, subservience to God's will, and serious self-scrutiny — to raise himself up to become the cherished partner and co-worker of His Creator. Alone among all of God's creation, this human being, formed from the lowly earth, is granted the Divine gift to take his very earth-ness and to transform it into a vehicle of holiness. King David gives expression to this in Psalm 8:

> .... When I behold Your heavens, the works of Your fingers,
> The moon and the stars which You have ordained —
> What is man that You are mindful of him?
> And the son of man that You visit him?
> Yet You have made him a little lower than the angels,
> And You crown him with glory and honor ....

It is this limitless possibility — to become almost as spiritual as an angel — that lies imbedded deep within that poignant and astounding question:

Shall I conceal from Abraham that which I intend to do?

N.B. In referring to God's question as one that He asks Himself, I am following the reading of Nahmanides and others at Genesis 18:7. Rashi's reading, as indicated at Genesis 1:24, would be that God asks the question not of Himself but of His heavenly court. In either reading, the power of the question is not diminished.

7

So the Lord said, "Because the outcry against Sodom and Amorah is so great, and because their sin is very grievous, I will go down now, and see if they have done according to the cry against them …. And Abraham drew near and said, "Will You also destroy the righteous with the wicked …?"

Genesis 18:20-23

 ## PROBING THE MYSTERY: WILL THE DIVINE JUDGE NOT DO JUSTICE?

It is an electrifying moment: Finite man fears that an act of his Infinite Creator might be construed as lacking in justice, and this man hurls a challenge at his God.

More electrifying it is that the Creator does not say to this man: "Who are you to challenge Me? So have I decided and so will it be." Instead, the Creator of all the universe engages this mortal creature in a dialogue.

Let us set the stage. In Genesis 18:20, God declares that He is about to destroy Sodom and Amorah because of their wickedness. In verses 23-25, Abraham approaches God and says:

"Will you destroy the righteous with the wicked? Perhaps there are fifty righteous people within the city. Far be it from You to destroy the righteous with the wicked. Hashofet kol ha-aretz lo ya-aseh mishpat? *Will the Judge of all the earth not do justice?"*

God accepts the challenge. He replies: If I find in Sodom fifty righteous people, I will not destroy the city.

Abraham responds: Perhaps there will be fifty minus five in the city?

God responds: I will not destroy the city if there are forty-five.

Abraham speaks yet again: Perhaps there will only be forty?

God says: I will not do it for the sake of the forty.

Abraham: Perhaps thirty?

God: I will not do it for the thirty.

Abraham asks for twenty, and God agrees.

He asks for ten, and God agrees.

At this point, God departs and the dialogue comes to an end.

The question of Abraham is the eternal question of the mortal man who does not comprehend the ways of the Lord. All the eternal questions are contained in this question, all the mortal inability to comprehend the ways of the Immortal, all the exquisite pain and longing and yearning that are engendered by this inability to comprehend:

Why do the righteous suffer?

Why do the wicked prosper?

Where is the justice that is supposed to govern the universe?

Why?

How?

Where?

Who?

What?

But most of all, Why?

It is man reaching out to touch his Maker, knowing all the time that He is untouchable.

It is man of dust and ashes — the very words that Abraham uses to describe himself in this dialogue with God — who is made of the dust and returns to the dust, who clamors upon the stage of life, and then is heard no more; whose body ultimately returns to the earth; who wishes to draw himself up from the ground and to become one with the One above.

[Note, incidentally, the difference between dust and ashes. Dust has no past, but it has a future: one can plant seeds in the dust of the earth, one can build in the dust of the earth. Ashes had a past — something had to burn in order to create them — but they have no future. To which aspect of dust and ashes does Abraham allude: Is he like the ash without a future and like the dust without a past? Or is he like the ash that had a past, and like the dust that still has a future? It is ambiguous.]

What is not ambiguous is that man who is transformed into ephemeral dust and ash nevertheless yearns to touch Him Who is eternal, Who is past, present, and future. Because this dust and ash, this mortal human being, is also created in the image of God, and his ultimate desire is to be united with He Who created him and to comprehend His mysterious ways.

The question of Abraham is not merely a request for information. It is a challenge directed at the Creator:

You Who are the embodiment of all that is good,
You Who wants His creatures to live justly,
You Who rewards the righteous and punishes the wicked —
will You now punish the righteous together with the wicked?
You Who are the essence of righteousness,
Who are the Judge of all the earth —
can it be that the essence of justice
will do a deed that contains the potential for injustice —
and not only injustice to Your creatures,
but also to Your Divine Name?

Abraham did not have to intercede on behalf of Sodom. He could have followed the precedent of his forebear, Noah, who, in the face of the impending destruction, not merely of one city but of all mankind, remained singularly and resolutely silent, accepting God's decree. But Abraham's anguish at the possibility that the Judge of all the earth would act unjustly is so profound that he has no alternative but to intercede. Abraham's challenge is echoed by Moses and Aaron: "Shall one man sin, and You rage against the whole community?" (Numbers 16:22)

Nor is it a half-hearted, perfunctory intercession. Abraham pursues and pleads and refuses to back down: fifty, forty-five, forty, thirty, twenty, ten. Six persistent attempts to strike a bargain with God.

The lives of the righteous are at stake, and Abraham is ready to stake his own life on their behalf, and on behalf of the idea of justice. And not only the lives of the righteous, but the lives of the wicked as well, for if the city does in fact contain the righteous few, it is not only those few who will be saved, but the entire city.

Abraham does not know how the Almighty will react to this earthly questioning of the ways of heaven. Perhaps Abraham will be punished for this presumptuous interrogation of his Creator. Perhaps his own life will now come to an end.

But the Creator, the Mighty One, the Cause of all things, is willing to enter into negotiations with His creature of dust and ashes — but who is also of the Image of the Creator. Because the Creator wants His creature to know that although the ways of Heaven are not always understood by those who are of dust and ashes, the ways of Heaven are not unjust, and the Judge of all the earth is in fact the God of justice.

Abraham, do you think for a moment that God does not know how many righteous men there are in Sodom?

Abraham knows that God knows. But Abraham wants to transmit several truths: first, that even when circumstances are bleak and without hope, the gates of prayer remain open to the genuine seeker. Abraham knows that God knows. But Abraham is here engaged in a prayer. And beyond the prayer, he wants to make it known to all men that they should not judge the Judge of all the earth too quickly.

Adam, Cain, Abraham.

Consider Adam, God's own handiwork. Adam violates God's trust and hides in fear, unable to answer the question, *Where are you?*

Consider Cain, son of Adam. He kills his brother, and to God's question he retorts in insolence, *Am I my brother's keeper?*

Consider Abraham, the friend of God, God's own beloved, from whom God does not withhold any of His plans. He does not violate God's word, he does not hide from God, and his question to God is born of lovingkindness, not arrogance. He knows where he is, and he knows where his brother is.

Abraham repairs the damage done by the transgression of Adam and by the question of Cain. It is no wonder that God Himself, when he announces his intentions to destroy Sodom, says to His ministering angels: "Can I conceal from Abraham that which I am about to do?" (Genesis 18:17). One does not conceal one's intentions from one's beloved.

Abraham's intercession on behalf of Sodom is the response to Cain's arrogant question: Yes, says Abraham, even when he is not literally our flesh and blood, we are all our brothers' keeper.

Isaac to his son: Who are you, my son?

Genesis *27:18*

Esau to Isaac: Have you only one blessing,
my father?

Genesis *27:38*

THE STRUGGLE FOR THE BLESSING:
▸ *WHO ARE YOU?*
▸ *HAVE YOU ONLY ONE BLESSING?*

A number of questions are found in the riveting
narrative of Isaac's blessing to his son (see Genesis
27). They are all significant, of course, but we will
look carefully at two of these questions — one that
Isaac addresses to his son, and one that Esau
addresses to his father Isaac.

I. Jacob is standing before his father, Isaac, in the disguise prepared by his mother, Rebecca. She is determined that Isaac's
blessing not be given to Esau, who, she knows, has succeeded in
disguising his true nature from his father. As Esau has disguised
himself for evil purposes, so does she now disguise Jacob for good
purposes. The blessing must at all costs go to Jacob, so that the

destiny and purity of the family and future people of Israel not be corrupted by Esau. Rebecca therefore disguises Jacob to appear to be his brother and to receive the coveted blessing from Isaac.

It should be easy to deceive Isaac: although he is in command of all of his formidable intellectual and spiritual capacities, the Torah, in introducing this blessing scene to us in Genesis 27, calls our attention to his old age and to his blindness:

> And it came to pass, when Isaac had become old, and his eyes dimmed from seeing, that he summoned Esau and said to him... See, now, I have aged....

Thus, even the most superficial disguise should be enough to make him think that this is Esau standing before him. Rebecca is confident that all will go well. Jacob is not so certain, but reluctantly and dutifully follows his mother's directives.

(Most remarkable here is that, among the Patriarchs, Jacob is the embodiment of the quality of emet/truth, as recorded in Micah 7:20: Titein emet l'Yaakov — *"Grant truth to Jacob...." The classic works of Jewish thought — including numerous Midrashim — describe Abraham as embodying the traits of Kindness and Benevolence* (chesed); *Isaac as the embodiment of Strength (gevurah) in the service of God; and Jacob as the blend of both, which is the quintessence of Truth (emet), since Truth requires the proper balance of all good qualities. Jacob and Rebecca are able to harness this quality into the service of an even higher truth: the need to preserve the integrity and destiny of the people of Israel, and to deliver her from the perversion and distortion embodied by Esau. One must also note, incidentally, that this is not a garden-variety deception. Clearly its success is a result of subtle intervention from Above. These very complex issues are the focus of much discussion among the classical Jewish sources, but are beyond the purview of this essay.)*

Jacob approaches his father and says one word: *Avi* — "my father." Isaac replies, *Hineni* — "Here am I." But then he adds the question: *Mi ata b'ni* — "Who are you, my son?" (Genesis

27:18). On one level, he might be asking, "Which of my sons are you?" On a deeper level, he might also be asking, "You who are my son, who are you really? What is your essence? Whoever you are, Jacob or Esau, do you know who you are?" Does Isaac suspect that something is not right? Jacob has uttered only one word: *Avi*.

Note that from verse 18, where Jacob first speaks to his father, through verse 27, just before the actual blessing begins — a span of ten verses — Isaac speaks seven different times. In these seven speeches, Isaac utilizes the term *b'ni* — "my son," — no less than eight times.

> V. 18: Who are you, my son?
> V. 20: You have found it so quickly, my son.
> V. 21: Come close, that I may feel you, my son, whether you be my son Esau or not.
> V. 24: You are my son Esau.
> V. 25: Bring it near to me and I will eat of my son's venison ...
> V. 26: Come near now, and kiss me, my son.
> V. 27: The aroma of my son is as the aroma of a field ...

It is a hidden refrain, not very obvious, heard only in the background, but if one listens carefully it echoes and resounds, like the beat of a hammer, like the pealing of a bell, again and again: *b'ni, b'ni,* — "my son, my son."

Does Isaac sense that something is amiss? Does he seek reassurance from someone, or from within himself? Does the repetition of *b'ni* stem from an inner doubt that keeps emerging and refuses to be silenced? Or is he simply delighting in the savor of the profound moment when he is about to transfer the heritage and the Godly blessing to his son, the offspring for whom he and Rebecca had prayed, and without whom there would be no future for the family destined to carry God's name to the world?

Even a cursory reading tilts the balance to the side of suspicion. With each succeeding response of Jacob, the father's concerns seem to deepen, until finally in verse 21 he comes out with it:

"Come near that I may feel you, my son, whether you be my son Esau or not." There it is, clear as the daylight: Isaac senses that something is not right, that perhaps the person standing before him is a pretender, that perhaps he is not Esau after all.

What is it that kindles Isaac's suspicions? Esau and Jacob are twins, and even their voices are identical. But there is apparently something in the words of Jacob that makes Isaac sense that perhaps this is not truly Esau standing before him. Is it a certain delicacy of tone, a certain innocence that was never there before? After all, Esau is a man of the field, a hunter, while Jacob is a dweller in tents, a contemplative student. A certain gruffness of tone in the voice of Esau was to be expected; refinement and delicacy would be most surprising. Or is it because it requires only one word for Jacob to betray his discomfort in the role he is being forced to play, and that Isaac senses that something is amiss? What is clear, however, is this: the mere utterance of the single word, *avi* — "my father," immediately triggers a question mark in the heart of Isaac. But it is not only the tone and quality of the voice; it is also the words themselves that puzzle the aged father. Esau is always duly respectful of his father, but words like "God" are not a normal part of his lexicon. And yet when his father wonders how he could have caught and prepared all that venison so rapidly, the response is that "the Lord thy God caused it to happen before me" (Genesis 27:21). At which point, Isaac asks his son to come closer so he can touch him and determine "if you are truly my son or not." And after he touches him he is still puzzled: "the voice is the voice of Jacob, but the hands are the hands of Esau."

Who are you? Who am I? It is a question that everyone must ask of himself constantly. Behind all our masks, beneath all the cosmetics that disguise our every move, one ultimate question must always be asked of one's self: *Mi ata* — "Who are you?" Do our actions match our words, or are we, too, bearers of the voice of Jacob who have the hands of Esau?

The Biblical questions are addressed not only to the Biblical personalities, but to each human being. Adam is asked, "Where are you?" (ibid. 3:9); Cain is asked, "Where is your brother?" (ibid. 4:9) Jacob is asked, "Who are you?" (ibid. 27:18). Jacob asks his son Joseph about Menashe and Efraim: "Who are these?" (ibid. 48:8) Rebecca asks herself, *Lama ze anochi* — "Why am I thus?" (ibid. 25:22); the stranger asks Joseph, "What do you seek?" (ibid. 37:15); Moses asks God, *Mi anochi* — "Who am I?" (Exodus 3:11); God asks Bil'am, "Who are these people with you?" (Numbers 22:9).

The questions Who? Where? Why? What? When? pervade the Torah. They also pervade the lives of sensitive people eternally.

Who are you really?
What is your essence?
What are you made of?
Do you know who you are?
Who are your children?
Do you know where your brother is?
What do you seek?
Who are your friends?
Do you know where you are now, where you were yesterday, where you will be tomorrow?

II. *A second substantive question is posed in this narrative.*

Through the stratagem engineered by his mother, Jacob has just received the coveted blessing from his father, who had intended to give this blessing to his other twin son, Esau. Just as Jacob departs the room, Esau enters and discovers that the blessing has been given to his brother. Esau cries bitter tears, Isaac trembles a great trembling (see further below), but nevertheless informs him that he has already given the blessing to someone else and cannot now give it to Esau. At which point Esau cries out: "Have you only one blessing, my father?" (Genesis 27:38).

This narrative, like life itself, contains tantalizing ambiguities.

What is the role of the blind and aged father Isaac? Is he simply being duped by Rebecca who manipulates things from behind the scenes, or does he have his own plans?

Why does Rebecca choose this convoluted means of obtaining the blessing for Jacob? If she has suspicions about Esau, why go through the elaborate charade? Why does she not simply speak about them to her husband Isaac? (See R' Naftali Tzvi Yehudah Berlin ["Netziv"] on Genesis 27 for a perceptive insight into the matter of Rebecca's relationship with Isaac.)

Most perplexing of all is the question asked by Esau.

How are we to understand Esau's begging, pleading and — literally — weeping for his father's blessing? Esau, who rejects all things spiritual, for whom the body is sovereign; who gives credence only to that which he can see and touch and taste and smell and hear; who lies and cheats and steals and rapes and murders; Esau the master of deception, the ultimate hypocrite — *Esau, why would you want a blessing from your aged father? Surely you do not believe that a blessing is as important as the hunt, as the red meat and the good wine? This blessing over which you are weeping — is this just another object you want to possess? What possible meaning could a blessing — which is only words, is beyond the physical, and presupposes some faith — have for you, who believe in nothing, who are the embodiment of selfishness and arrogance, and whose primary goal in life is to satisfy your appetites and lusts as quickly and as frequently as possible? Or is this another example of your devious cunning? Do you want to impress upon your father, even now, that you are a righteous person, and so you shed false tears about a spiritual matter that means nothing to you? Is this the ultimate deception of one who would plunder and ravage in the fields and then return home and sanctimoniously engage his father in discussions about the esoteric requirements of tithing?* (See Rashi at Genesis 25:27, citing *Midrash Tanhuma*.)

An understandable accusation — but even an Esau can be unjustly accused. In this instance, Esau is not engaged in duplicity. He truly wants his father's blessing. The cry, "Do you have but one blessing, my father?" and everything else that Esau utters in this scene — his loud and bitter wailing, the twice-uttered plea, "Bless me also, my father" — all bear the unmistakable imprint of a genuine *cri de coeur*. Here there is no hypocrisy, no cunning.

Esau's lament defies understanding only if we view Esau as a one-dimensional creature of evil. Certainly he fits the stereotype: he is born as hairy as an adult, and his coloring is red, the color of sin. ["If your sins be like scarlet ...." (Isaiah 1:18)] The Torah describes him as a "man who knows the hunt, a man of the field," contrasting him with his twin brother Jacob who is a "simple man, a dweller in tents." And he is in fact a great sinner.

But to paint Esau without any redeeming qualities whatsoever would be a caricature. For one thing, Esau was very careful about the duties of honoring one's father, and he honored Isaac to the maximum degree possible. In fact, Rabbi Shimon ben Gamliel says that although he himself greatly stressed the honor due to his own parents, it is as nothing when compared to the honor which Esau rendered his father, Isaac (see *Bereshit Rabbah* 65:16; *Devarim Rabbah* 1:15). For example, whenever Esau went in to serve his father in some way, he always dressed in his princely clothing, because one does not dress in an ordinary way when in the presence of greatness.

That an Esau could recognize the greatness and saintliness of Isaac suggests that there was more to Esau than an evil that was unrelievedly black. And the plaintive cry, "Do you have but one blessing?" is an eminently logical one: you who are so saintly and heavenly, whose entire being is spiritual, surely you possess more than one blessing to share with your sons!

Strange and surprising though it may seem, there is apparently a bond between them, an odd affinity between father and son. Perhaps this is because Isaac, who has never quite returned fully to this earthly existence following his experience as the sacrificial lamb on Moriah, feels a special intimacy toward this son who is so physical and so earthly, so much his very opposite. Could it be that he sees in Esau a means that would make it possible for Isaac to better comprehend the ways of this earth? And does Esau feel a similar pull towards his own opposite, the spiritual realm that Isaac embodies? Can it be that Esau sees in Isaac the means by which Esau might better understand the ways of Heaven?

Or is it possible that Isaac sees in Esau's elemental power and energy, once it is channeled, a potential generator for holiness even more far-reaching than Jacob's? And does he want to give Esau his eternal blessing in the hope that this will effect the sea change so needed to transform his son into the force which will ensure the eternity of the Jewish people? This could underlie the eight-fold repetition of *b'ni* — "my son" — a term of endearment and affection — which we noted above.

And, for his part, could it be that Esau seeks this blessing because he knows he is deeply enmeshed in terrible things and really wants to escape them, and believes that his father's blessing will help him loosen the net of evil in which he is trapped? In a word, is Esau having second thoughts, and does he sense that with his father's blessing he might effect some measure of repentance, and that without it he will sink ever deeper into the pit? Are his tears brought on by genuine regret and remorse? *Surely you can grant me the blessing which will yet save me from my precipitous slide into the netherworld.*

Evil is complex, not a simple matter of black and white. Even the most evil among men, after all, possesses a soul that emanates from a Divine source. That soul cannot be entirely suppressed and contained, and it surfaces in different ways. Certainly it is so with Esau who is, after all, the offspring of Isaac and Rebecca, and the grandson of Abraham and Sarah, and within whom there exists the seed of religious greatness. He possesses a profound spiritual power, but it has been diverted to evil purposes. Esau's latent power is evident in the comment of *Midrash Yalkut Shim'oni, Toledot* 115, that tells how the Jewish people ultimately suffers greatly as a direct result of the three tears that Esau shed. And that even an Esau is capable of repentance is evidenced by the Sages' comment that if Jacob's daughter Dinah had been permitted to marry Esau, she might have brought him back to holiness (*Midrash Rabbah* 76:9, commenting on Genesis, *Sidrah Vayishlach;* cited by Rashi, Genesis 32:23).

In this reading, Isaac is not the blind old father who is deceived by Esau. He knows Esau for what he is, but he also perceives that Esau bears a certain power within him that, once tamed, can be utilized for good and holiness, and perhaps he hopes that the blessing will propel him into the path of righteousness.

That Isaac could entertain such beliefs about an evil son is not surprising. Isaac, after all, is Abraham's son who willingly sacrifices himself on Mount Moriah. For him, evil is ephemeral. His *Akeida* experience has blinded him not only physically; it has rendered him unable to see the reality of evil. Since that moment, he has been an unworldly creature, not engaged in the affairs of ordinary mortals. Rebecca, on the other hand, knows her son from another dimension. She hears in him the echo of her own brother Laban and the resonance of her unholy family — a family that equipped her to recognize evil when she sees it, and taught her how to do battle with it.

During the blessing scene it is evident, as we have seen, that Isaac is not at all convinced that the son standing before him is in fact Esau. He clearly senses that something is amiss. We have already noted the gradual but unmistakable unfolding of Isaac's inner doubts.

As we listen to Isaac's deepening misgivings, it becomes clear to us that not only does Isaac suspect he is being fooled, even more apparent is the fact that Isaac wants to be absolutely certain that it is in fact his son Esau and no one else who receives the blessing.

Isaac here risks everything with this one blessing. He has no fear that Jacob will be anything but a holy person; Jacob represents Heaven, and that will always be his domain and that of his descendants. But Isaac has it in his power to create a heaven on earth. Esau, once his evil power can be channeled into good, bears a vast and untapped potential for holiness in this world. With one phrase, Isaac can capture both heaven and earth forever, and not only Jacob, but also Esau can be harnessed into the service of God. This is why Isaac must be certain that this son standing before him is in fact that primordial force who is Esau, who, though he is now evil, will be transformed into good.

Rebecca perceives reality differently. She has seen evil, has lived with it all her life. Until the end of days, evil, whether within oneself or within the world, will not be redeemed or transformed into good by a simple blessing, even one that emanates from the spiritual power of an Isaac. Evil must be tenaciously fought and decisively defeated. This is implicit in the prophecy Rebecca receives before the twins are born: ... *ul'om mil'om ye-ematz, v'rav ya'avod tza'ir* — "... and the one nation shall be stronger than the other, and the elder will serve the younger" (Genesis 25:23) — a prophecy she apparently never shares with her husband Isaac. In this earthly world there will be no happy partnership between Jacob and Esau.

The struggle over who shall receive the blessing is thus not only between the twin sons, but also between husband and wife. Rebecca knows well the deep fissures and pitfalls of this world, while Isaac knows only the spiritual realm of the beyond and the Above. Thus it is not surprising that Rebecca never shares with her husband the prophecy about Jacob's superior merit, nor her fears about their son Esau. Isaac does not see this world as it is, but as it should be. And at the ultimate moment of truth, when decisive action must be taken lest the blessing be given to evil, she takes resolute, this-worldly, single-minded action to defeat Esau with his own weapon: deception. For she knows beyond any doubt that in this world the hands of Esau will never be reconciled with the voice of Jacob.

When Esau appears and demands his blessing, and Isaac realizes what has occurred, he "trembles a great trembling" (ibid. 27:33). We are not quite certain why.

Does he remember that morning long ago when, on the way to the *Akeida*, he had called out to his father, *Avi* — "My father," and his father had answered, *Hineni b'ni,* — "Here I am, my son," — and when Isaac thereupon asked his father that if they were going to offer a sacrifice, he saw all the tools of an offering, but where was the lamb? And does Isaac now recall that his father had answered only cryptically that God would show them the lamb? And does he think of this because he had now called out to his own son, *B'ni* — My son, and his son had also answered, *Hineni* but did not answer his question fully? Does Isaac now realize that just as his father had done what had to be done without Isaac's knowledge, so now his son has done to him what has to be done, again without his knowledge?

Does Isaac tremble a great trembling because he now perceives that God has somehow taken matters out of his hands and seen to it that Jacob receives the blessing after all, and that his dream of transforming Esau from without is not destined to be? Perhaps Isaac now recognizes with sudden clarity that Esau his son will remain evil until he redeems himself from within through his internal and personal struggle; that so it must be in this world of reality, and therefore Isaac trembles at what might have been; that in this world he might have unwittingly reinforced Esau's titanic evil beyond any redemption. Rebecca's view of reality, Isaac must now acknowledge, is the more perceptive, the more discerning.

"Have you but one blessing, my father?"

Yes, Esau, I possess but one blessing; it is a blessing that permits one to dominate the physical and not be dominated by it; to master that which is on this earth, and not be mastered by it. But now I know that this blessing is not suitable for you. I will bless you with physical dominion over the earth — but spiritual dominion I cannot grant you. To achieve this, you alone will have to struggle with the evil within you. May God grant you the realization that evil has to be subdued and defeated; that it cannot be transformed without conflict, whether within the world or within one's own self; and that no one else but you yourself can save you from your slide into the netherworld.

After all is said and done, this story could be told only about twins, for we are each twins within ourselves, a fusion of Esau and Jacob, earth and heaven, body and spirit. We possess the Voice, which bears no physical entity — the Voice of Jacob. And we also possess the Hands, which are physical and which bend matter to our will — the Hands of Esau. Within each person there exists both the Esau pulling us down toward the earth, and the Jacob lifting us up toward Heaven. *Mi ata?* — "Who are you?" is the question of our father Isaac — and the question of our Father above. Esau and Jacob, earth and heaven, cannot live as equals. "The older [stronger] one will serve the younger [weaker] one" (ibid. 25:23). One must dominate the other; never can they be ascendant or descendant at the same time, as stated in Talmud *Megillah* 6a concerning Jerusalem and Rome: "if this one is filled, the other is laid waste; if the other one is filled, this one is laid waste." (See also Rashi on Genesis 25:23.) This is the truth that this gripping and mysterious incident brings home to us — as suggested by the two key questions subtly embedded within its multi-layered folds.

9

And it happened ... that the butler
of the king of Egypt and the baker ...
were put into the dungeon,
the place where Joseph was confined ...
And the two of them dreamed a dream ....
And Joseph came to them in the morning,
and looked upon them, and behold, they were sad.
And he asked...
Why do you look so sad today?

Genesis 40:1-6

THE CARING MAN IN THE DUNGEON: *WHY DO YOU LOOK SO SAD TODAY?*

In a dungeon there is no time for niceties or pleasantries. Each prisoner is occupied with his own fate, his own anger and resentment, his own certainty of his innocence and persecution, his own schemes for getting out. Nothing exists for him outside his own self. The numbing routine of prison life has robbed him, and each person around him, of all individuality. Officials, jailers, other inmates — the sum of his daily human contact — are nothing more than ciphers and robots, lifeless automatons performing their daily tasks, who are no more significant than a fly on the wall, a roach on the floor.

This makes Joseph's conversation with Pharaoh's chief butler and chief baker all the more remarkable. "Joseph came into them in the morning and looked upon them, and behold they were sad." Joseph, himself a prisoner, has by now been elevated to the position of overseer of the other prisoners. But instead of lording it over them, he clearly looks upon them as fellow human beings; he actually takes note of them, and he sees that the butler and the baker are out of sorts — even more than is normal for the inhabitants of a dungeon.

This is itself a startling change in prison behavior: that anyone should take note of anyone else. Joseph could have dismissed it and gone about his daily work. But Joseph has noticed distraught human beings and must come to their help, and so he takes the initiative and asks a fateful question: "Why do you look so sad today?"

The sequence of events is important. First, in 40:6, Joseph "saw them and behold, they were unhappy." And then comes Joseph's inquiry. It is indeed a fateful question, because had he not asked it, had he ignored the sad countenance of the two prisoners, Joseph would have languished in the dungeon, might never have interpreted Pharaoh's dreams, might never have become the powerful viceroy of Egypt, and might not have saved the ancient world from famine. But he did ask the question, he did express concern, and that made all the difference.

Note the specificity of Joseph's question. Not simply a vague and general, "How are you doing today?" or "Good morning," or "How are you?" — any of which, to be sure, would have been a welcome expression of human interaction. Joseph goes far beyond generalities: *I notice that you look sad today; is something troubling you?* (There is here, incidentally, an echo of God's words to Cain in Genesis 4:6: *Lamah naflu fanecha* — "Why are you crestfallen?"; and a foreshadowing of the Talmudic dictum to greet everyone, as embodied in the conduct of the Sages, particularly Rabbi Yochanan ben Zakai, who was always the first to greet everyone he saw. As *Berachot* 17a puts it: "No one ever greeted him first ...."

To notice the other; to see the other; to express concern for the other, this is the distinguishing characteristic of Joseph. As a child of seventeen, he notices that the children of the maidservants are not being fairly treated by his brothers, and so he comes to their defense. He notices, he sees, he acts. On the dangerous mission to find his wandering brothers, the stranger asks him what he seeks, and Joseph replies, *Et achai anochi mevakesh* — "My brothers do I seek" (Genesis 15-16). Constantly seeking his brothers; constantly concerned for his fellow man: this is Joseph. He is the ultimate provider in whose hands lies the welfare of millions of people of the ancient world who are starving during the seven-year famine. This selfsame Joseph, most powerful man in Egypt, will not embarrass his brothers before his courtiers, and so, when he finally reveals himself to his brothers, he dispatches everyone else from the throne room (ibid. 45:1):

> *Joseph could not restrain himself in the presence of all who stood before him, so he called out: Remove every one from before me! Thus no one remained with him when Joseph made himself known to his brothers.*

Truly to see another human being: this is the essence of being human. Perhaps it is this very concern for his fellow human being that helps unravel one of the great mysteries about Joseph. This most beloved child of Jacob is sent by his father to find his brothers (Genesis 37:14). He never returns home. He is thrown into a pit, sold to the wandering Ishmaelites, who in turn sell him to the house of Potiphar as a slave, where he is condemned to the dungeon on trumped-up charges (based on his refusal to violate the trust of his master and the dictates of his God (ibid. 39:38), and from there he is rescued because of his ability to read dreams accurately, and he becomes the viceroy of Egypt. In total, he is gone from his home and from his beloved father for twenty-two years. He has never forgotten his father, whose image he sees regularly before him (*Sotah* 36b).

How is it that in all this time he does not send a single message to tell his aged father that he is still alive? Surely as the most powerful man in Egypt he had the wherewithal to get a message back to Canaan!

It is a vexing question, one that disturbs all who study the text. Perhaps a key to understanding the strange silence of Joseph is this very concern for others that marks his entire life. Quite possibly, he is fearful that if he communicates with his father, his father will certainly learn the true facts of the matter — even if Joseph does not relate all the details of what his brothers did to him.

Rather than risk unleashing the wrath of Jacob upon his brothers, Joseph elects to remain silent, as anguished as that silence is for him.

Buttressing this silence is his knowledge that the dreams that so enraged his brothers were not mere dreams but were actually prophecies. Joseph knows that as an instrument of Divine prophecy, he must do nothing that might interfere with the gradual unfolding of the delicate rose of these prophetic dreams.

Rather, let them slowly unwind, let them become realized, and in the fullness of time all will fall into place. (Cf. Nachmanides at Genesis 42:9)

There are others on this earth. Our task as human beings is to learn to relate to and to interact and to live with all these others. To live as if we were all alone, as if there were only the self and nothing beyond the self, is the literal definition of selfishness. There is an entire body of Torah, *bein adam lachaveiro*, that deals with interpersonal relationships — half of the Ten Commandments is devoted to the subject — whose purpose is to help us transcend our innate self-centeredness and to remind us that we are not alone on this earth.

There is an additional purpose to *bein adam lachaveiro*: to combat the loneliness that is our lot. Everyone is lonely and in need of attention and care, even when he or she lives among tens of thousands. To take notice of the other, to recognize the other, assuages the loneliness of myself and of the other. If only the self exists and no other, then life becomes unbearable, and there is no existence either for the self or for the other. The interpersonal regulations of the Torah teach us that no man is an island unto himself. The Torah's rules instruct us how to create bridges between the islands, to connect them, and to make them as one.

"Why do you look so sad today?" asked Joseph, and in so doing he affected the course of history.

Concern with the welfare of the other can change history — both of the other and of one's own self.

10

And Joseph could not restrain himself
before all those that stood before him ....
And no man stood with him
when Joseph made himself known to his brothers ....
And Joseph said:
I am Joseph,
Does my father still live?

Genesis 45:1-3

The Things That Matter:
Does My Father Still Live?

In the wrenching reunion of Joseph and his brothers, the very first words that Joseph utters after he reveals his true identity are a question: *Ani Yoseph, ha-od avi chai* — "I am Joseph; does my father still live?" (Genesis 45:3).

This, of course, is not the first time Joseph has inquired after his father. Chapter 43 describes an earlier meeting between Joseph and the brothers. After their first visit to Egypt, they had brought back provisions to the homestead and to their aged father Jacob in Canaan. When they return to Egypt, Joseph invites them to dine with him. During this meal, Joseph asks an apparently casual question, but one which in actuality is of primary concern to him: "Is your old father well, of whom you spoke? Is he still alive?" (ibid. 43:27).

There is in this question a logical inconsistency. Ordinarily, one asks first if someone is alive, and only later if he is well. But Joseph reverses the order.

Clearly, Joseph wants to determine if his father is still alive. But perhaps he does not want to raise any suspicions in the minds of his brothers, who might well wonder why this viceroy of Egypt is so concerned about their old father. So instead of telegraphing this primary concern of his, Joseph disguises it in conversational banter in which there is no need to be precise or logical. Is he well? Is he alive? The question about being alive comes across as an after-thought, a polite inquiry. This could be Joseph's way of disarming his guests, of making them think that it is simply a casual, socially correct question, like "How are you?"

This question stands in stark contrast with the same question that Joseph asks later in chapter 45, when he finally reveals himself. There, he makes no effort to conceal his anxiety. He is their long-lost brother, and the question comes like a hammer blow, unsubtle and direct: "I am Joseph; does my father still live?" No longer is it necessary to mask his concerns.

The question demonstrates, obviously, that foremost in the heart of Joseph is his affection and his longing for his father. In the life of a human being there are various relationships: with God, with spouse and children, with fellow human beings, and with one's father and mother. This parental relationship, together with the others, is codified and given flesh in the Ten Commandments. But even before the Commandments, Joseph represents not merely the respect and honor due to parents in general, but also the affection and the devotion which are unique to the relationship between this son and this father. When the text says, for example, that Joseph was the child of Jacob's old age (Genesis 37:3), the Midrash informs us that, of all his sons, Jacob chose to teach only Joseph all the wisdom that he had learned at the feet of Isaac and Abraham (*Bereishit Rabbah* 84:8), for Jacob saw Joseph as the bearer of the destiny of the people of Israel. The bond between father and son was strong, just as was the bond between Jacob and Rachel, the mother of Joseph.

When Jacob sends Joseph on the journey to seek out his brothers in Shechem, both father and son know that not only the lonely journey, but also the meeting with the openly hostile brothers is beset with peril. And yet, without any hesitation, without any expression of fear or doubt, Joseph responds to his father's request with one word: *Hineni* — "Here I am," and he sets out on the fateful journey. His father asks him to go; he goes.

That the influence of his father Jacob remains paramount in the mind of Joseph even after he is sold into slavery is evident when he becomes the overseer of the house of Potiphar. The wife of Potiphar attempts to seduce Joseph, but Joseph sees before him the visage of his father and resists the temptation (*Sotah* 36b).

It is thus not surprising that after twenty-two years of absence the first words to emerge from the mouth of Joseph to his brothers should be a question about his father. But the strange apposition of part one — "I am Joseph" — and part two — "Does my father still live?" — strongly suggests that there are several layers of meaning beneath the surface of this question.

Is it an expression of incredulity? *I do not believe that he is still alive considering all that he has had to endure.*

Or is Joseph seeking reassurance about his father's welfare? *Yes, you have already told me that he lives, but now that you know who I am, tell me the full truth: is he in fact still alive?*

Is it an expression of unmitigated joy? *Assure me once again, for I can hardly believe it — is my father truly still alive?*

On a deeper level, Joseph's question is connected to the fact, alluded to above, that Joseph and his father are inextricably linked together. As we have seen, it was not simple parental favoritism that underlay Jacob's preference for Joseph, but prophetic considerations of Jewish destiny. Jacob without Joseph has no mooring. Thus, Jacob would not be consoled or comforted, and never ceased to mourn for his lost son (Genesis 37:35).

And Joseph, for his part, is inextricably bound to his father. Joseph without his father is not Joseph. Thus the words, "I-am-Joseph-does-my-father-still-live," are logically connected; they are said in one breath, like a first name and a last name. Joseph's very life is a positive response to the question, Does my father still live? The awareness that he must remain the embodiment of his father's livingness has been the spiritual identification card that Joseph has carried with him through all these twenty-two years. It is this which has kept him loyal to the ideals of the family of Israel despite his trials as a slave and despite the temptations of royal power. It is thus reasonable that, when he identifies himself to his brothers, Joseph's first words to them should be a question as to whether their lives also represent a similar positive response about their father, Jacob.

Note Joseph's significant choice of pronoun. He does not say "our father," but "my father." Is this a subtle rebuke to the brothers who did not behave towards Jacob as to a beloved father, who callously lied to him and encouraged him to believe that his beloved Joseph had been torn apart by wild beasts? And since they also did not act towards Joseph as a brother, Joseph omits for now that description of himself: he does not say, "I am Joseph your brother," but simply, "I am Joseph ...."

Thus, Joseph's question is being asked not so much on a biological level as on a spiritual level: *I am still the son of my father. For me, his teachings are still alive. Are his teachings still alive for you? Are we still a family of destiny? Are we still the twelve brothers who will form the foundation stone of the eternal people that will spread the teachings of the One God to all of mankind? And as for your cruel treatment of him, have you changed yourselves enough so that he can once again become "our father" and not just "my father?"*

The brothers do not respond to the question. And yet, in verse 9, without waiting for an answer, Joseph instructs them to return to Canaan and to bring their father down to Egypt — even though they have not assured him that his father in fact still lives. That the brothers do not respond might be an indication that they grasp the subtle undertones of Joseph's question.

We have discussed in the previous chapter the constraints that might have prevented Joseph from communicating with his father during the previous twenty-two years: Joseph's fear of aborting the outcome of his prophetic dreams; the implications for the ultimate destiny of the people of Israel should Jacob ever learn the truth of what happened to Joseph. In fact, even after the dreams reach their culmination and Joseph finally reveals himself to his brothers, he still does not inform his father of what actually took place.

After all this, it is little wonder that the first words that explode from Joseph's lips when he reveals himself are those that have been bottled up for all these years. Does my father still live? — the father who has been uppermost in my mind since I was forcibly removed from him; the father who entrusted me with the destiny of the people of Israel; the father who loved me and loved my mother Rachel; the father who surely never ceased mourning for me: truly my father.

It was in fact over the affections of this father that the envy and suspicions of the brothers were first aroused. The brothers saw in Joseph an imposter, the latest in the line of earlier family imposters who had also tried to curry favor with their fathers, and who threatened to destroy the Jewish future. Their great-grandfather Abraham had been deceived by Ishmael, and only his wife Sarah had seen beneath the hypocritical exterior of Ishmael; their grandfather Isaac had been deceived by Esau, and only his wife Rebecca had perceived Esau's true self. Now their own father Jacob had a Joseph — but this time there was no wife to point out the truth to Jacob, for Rachel had died years earlier. Leah could not do it, because she would have been perceived as acting to favor her own sons over those of her dead sister. So the brothers did what they were convinced they had to do: they forcibly removed this pretender from their midst.

Now Joseph asks the question which will lay the matter to rest:

This father whose affections you were convinced were misguided, this father who seriously considered my dreams, this father who was always the central figure in our lives — is the figure of this father still a barrier between us?

Does this father, who you were certain was being deceived by me, still live in your hearts?

Is this father now someone whose judgments and decisions you are ready to follow?

Is my integrity and my honesty and my openness still an issue in your relationship with him, or have the years given you a newer perspective on my father — and on me?

Does my father, in all of the many nuances of this term, in all the remorse and regrets and remembrances which it evokes, still live?

Let us, however, examine the mysterious question from another perspective.

Note the precise point at which Joseph interrupts the eloquent pleading of his brother Judah. What is the last word which Judah utters before Joseph interrupts? It is the word *avi* — "my father." Judah has been pleading with Joseph to take into account the suffering of their aged father. If the young Benjamin is not permitted to return to Canaan, it will all but kill their father. He offers himself as a slave in the place of Benjamin.

Judah speaks a total of seventeen searing sentences. In these seventeen sentences, he mentions his father no less than fourteen times. It is after the fourteenth reference — "perchance I will see the evil that will befall my father" (verse 34) — that Joseph can no longer contain himself and cries out to his brothers: "I am Joseph; does my father still live?"

Why at this point? Because Judah's speech is the last act in the drama of reconciliation. It convinces Joseph finally that the quality that was so odious in his brothers — their insensitivity to the anguish of their father and brother when they sold Joseph into slavery — has now been repaired and corrected: Judah is so concerned about the impact on the father that he offers to go into slavery himself in order to save his father and his brother Benjamin.

Twenty-two years earlier, the leader of the brothers, Judah, son of Leah, had sold Joseph, son of Rachel, into slavery; now this same Judah is willing to ransom with his own life his youngest brother Benjamin, the other son of Rachel, from slavery. At this point Joseph knows that the story has come full circle, and that the brothers are different now from what they were then. Thus, Joseph's first words to them, focused on "my father," are engendered by Judah's last words to him, "my father." The father who long ago had become the dividing point between them has now become the unifying force between them. The word *avi* becomes the bridge of reconciliation between Joseph and his brothers.

And perhaps another search now reaches its completion as well. Recall that when Joseph first sets out on the journey on which his father has sent him, he wanders in the fields near Shechem in search of his brothers. A stranger appears to him and asks a question: *Mah tevakesh* — "What do you seek?" Joseph responds: "My brothers do I seek," which is literally true. But Joseph is searching not only for his physical brothers; he is searching for the brotherliness of brothers that has been lacking in their lives. In this reading, Joseph is answering the peculiar locution of the questioner: not *mi tevakesh* — "whom do you seek?" but *mah tevakesh* — "what do you seek?" He seeks not only his brothers, but the idea of brotherliness. Now, twenty-two years later, his search comes to an end: he finds the brothers, and the brotherliness, that he was seeking.

Joseph is the embodiment of the commandment "Love thy neighbor as thyself" (Leviticus 19:18). One cannot fulfill this requirement until he becomes aware that he has a neighbor. If, in his life, his neighbor is invisible and does not exist, then loving one's neighbor is only an empty phrase. The purpose of this phrase is first to remind us that there are others on this earth, and that our task as human beings is to see them, to become aware of them, and then to make the effort — not always a simple task — to love them.

Could this be the meaning of Joseph's singular outburst? Perhaps it is not a question at all, but an exclamation: Now I see that my father does in fact live, that the love and concern which he tried to teach us, and without which we cannot become the eternal people, still endures. Not "Does my father still live?" but "My father lives!"

Two questions are constantly asked of each individual:

1) *What do you seek?* What is it that is most valuable to you as you go through life; for what are you willing to surrender everything?

2) *Does my father still live?* Do my heritage, my sacred traditions, my Father in heaven, still exist for me? Do these teachings still play a role in my life?

If the answer is clearly affirmative, then the question becomes an exclamation of joy: despite everything that has transpired, my father still lives!

11

… And the brothers said:
Forgive the sin of your brothers ….
And Joseph wept when they spoke to him
And the brothers fell down before him and said:
We will be your slaves …
And Joseph said: Fear not,
for am I in place of God?

Genesis 50: 15-19

And Moses and Aaron said to Pharaoh,
Thus has said the Lord, God of Israel:
Let My people go
That they may worship Me …
And Pharaoh said:
Who is God
That I should hearken to His voice?

Exodus 5: 1-2

 ## OUT OF EGYPT, TWO VOICES:
▸ AM I IN PLACE OF GOD?
▸ WHO IS GOD?

Two voices resonate from Egypt. One is the voice of Joseph, the viceroy of Egypt. The second is that of Pharaoh, the enslaver of the Israelites. Although they did not know each other — "there arose a new king over Egypt, who knew not Joseph" (Exodus 1:8)

— the two voices represent a dispute that eternally spans the generations, until our very day. Each represents a credo of man's relationship to a Supreme Being.

Their father Jacob has died, and the brothers of Joseph are fearful that Joseph, now the powerful viceroy of Egypt, will take revenge upon them for what they did to him thirty-nine years earlier. Joseph attempts to reassure them that everything that has occurred was all part of God's eternal plan. And then he adds: Have no fear; *hatachat Elo-him anochi* — "Am I in place of God?" (Genesis 50:19).

The later Pharaoh's question to Moses, "Who is God?" offers a striking counterpoint to Joseph's question. Pharaoh is convinced that he himself is a god; therefore, he does not recognize any other deity, nor does he take seriously any claims to divinity other than his own. And even if there are divinities in other parts of the world, says Pharoah, they should limit themselves to their own land. Who is this divinity of Moses and Aaron who invades my territory and orders me to free my slaves? Yes, says Pharoah, here I am in the place of all gods.

Joseph, by contrast, knows that there is only one God, and no human being, no matter how powerful, can assume the position of a god. It is not for mortal man to exact retribution or revenge; only He can grant forgiveness for transgressions against Him.

Rashi elucidates and expands the words of Joseph:

> *It is obvious that though you intended to harm me, God transformed those intentions into something that was beneficial for everyone. Were I to take my revenge against you now, I would be acting against God's ultimate plan. Am I, then, in place of* Elo-him — *God?*

That Joseph's attachment to God is not merely a figure of speech designed to hearten his fearful brothers is underscored by his words of many years earlier. The earlier Pharaoh had experienced a disturbing series of dreams which no one could interpret. He is informed that in the Egyptian royal dungeon there is a young Hebrew lad who has the ability to interpret dreams accurately. Pharaoh sends for Joseph and says to him, "I have heard say of you that you can understand a dream to interpret it" (*Genesis* 41:15). Joseph immediately demurs: *Bil'adai* — "It is not I;" *Elo-him* — "God — shall give Pharaoh a favorable answer."

Here is a defining moment in the life of Joseph, a staggering opportunity for the young prisoner to ingratiate himself with the great monarch and to impress him with his (Joseph's) unique abilities. Instead, Joseph refuses to take credit for the gift that God has given him.

Thus, whether he is a lonely, forgotten prisoner, or whether he is the heralded and feared virtual monarch of Egypt, Joseph's faith and subservience to his God is manifest in every circumstance. Add to this the fact that Joseph was a strikingly handsome man, so much so that whenever Joseph's chariot passed through the streets of Egypt, the women would climb to the tops of the parapets and toss their jewelry at him in hopes that he might favor them with a glance. [See Rashi at Genesis 49:22, and *Pirke d'R Eliezer* 39.] As a powerful and attractive monarch, Joseph had much reason to be haughty and proud.

Not only is Joseph's self-effacing question the direct antidote to Pharaoh's arrogance; it is also a response to a phrase uttered by Joseph's father, Jacob. For even before Joseph was born, the identical Hebrew phrase appears in Genesis 30:2. The childless Rachel says to Jacob:

> Give me children, or else I die. Jacob's anger flared against Rachel, and he said: Hatachat Elo-him anochi — "Am I in place of God...?"

The text does not record them, so one can only imagine the earlier agonizing discussions on this subject between Jacob and Rachel. For it is not only Rachel who is eager to bear children; Jacob, too, wants children with Rachel. It was Rachel and not

Leah for whom he labored so many years at the house of Laban, because he saw prophetically that only through the offspring of Rachel will the destiny of Israel be assured. This outburst between husband and wife is surely the culmination of many earlier discussions. Finally, Rachel, in utter desperation, tells her husband that since he is a man of God, and has experienced directly the Presence of God throughout his life, he must present her case before the Almighty. In response, Jacob informs Rachel that he has in fact never ceased praying in her behalf, but that his prayers have been rejected, and that there is no more that he can do for her. He is not, after all, the Creator of the universe.

It is a reasonable position, but the Torah attests that he said it in anger. This response to his suffering wife must have been very hurtful to her. This, say our Sages, is not how a husband should talk to his wife (*Bereshit Rabbah* 71:7).

Even though Rachel does subsequently bear two sons, the words do not disappear. They hang in the air, throbbing with hurt and pain, uncorrected and unredeemed. Unredeemed, that is, until Joseph, the son of Jacob and Rachel, corrects the words, gives them a *tikkun,* pulls them down from their position of accusatory hovering and uses them in a loving way.

The same words, the same syllables, the same sounds: uttered in one way, they can maim and injure; uttered in another way, they can heal.

Joseph's humble "Am I in place of God?" and the later Pharaoh's arrogant "Who is God?" are two voices that are the reverse echoes of one another, and in fact symbolize two worldviews. Joseph's words establish the sole authority of the Creator; they resonate down through the centuries, across time and space. Pharaoh's words are the antithesis of Joseph's, and they resonate alongside his.

Pharaoh and Joseph: the two great leaders of ancient Egypt, the two great prototypes of how a man chooses to look at God. In Pharaoh's pantheon there is no room for another god, since he considers himself to be the master of all things. For Joseph, there is no pantheon at all. There is only the One God, and any mortal who would take for himself that role is a fool.

The power of Pharaoh's question should not be underestimated; its influence did not come to an end when his men and his chariots were drowned in the sea. The seeds of his refusal to recognize that there is a Sovereign above him who does in fact command him to do this and not to do that — these seeds were not drowned or destroyed. They remain embedded within the world, and within each human being.

We concede that God has the right to cross the threshold into our personal territory. But this is only a theory that we accept very reluctantly. We constantly strive to break out from the restrictions which it represents. Not only do individuals strive to break away, but also entire groups, entire peoples.

The words of the battle cry are different each time, but each time it is the same: Who is God? I am in charge of me, no one else has a right to tell me what to do or how to behave. I am the owner of my body; I am the ruler of my mind; I am the sovereign over my desires and my appetites. I am willing to recognize God's greatness, but He must not impinge on my personal domain or on my personal rights. Granted, there is a God, but He must not cross over the boundary lines into my territory and instruct me how to conduct my life.

It is a story as old as mankind. Listen carefully to the words of the cunning serpent as he whispers into Eve's ear. Eve had told him that the fruit of the tree in the middle of the Garden is forbidden, to which the serpent replies: "God knows that on the day you eat thereof, your eyes will be opened, and you will be as God, knowing good and evil" (Genesis 3:5).

The serpent's words are mysterious. What does he mean? What specifically is "knowing good and evil"?

He is saying that good and evil, right and wrong, are the key elements of life. Good leads to light and joy and bliss; evil leads to darkness and misery and destruction. He who can recognize what they are and can distinguish between them wields unlimited power over all of mankind, for he alone determines whether our every deed and our every word is good or evil, right or wrong.

But what is good and what is evil? They are so intermingled and intertwined, and the differences between them so blurred, that no mortal creature is able to distinguish between them and to define them. But whoever does possess this knowledge and this determination — whoever is able to define what is good and what is evil — holds in his hands the secret of life. At present, this secret and this knowledge are in the exclusive hands of God. He alone determines what is good and what is evil.

But, whispers the serpent, you now have the opportunity to obtain that knowledge for yourself. And once you obtain it, the power over all of life is yours, and you will become as God. Moreover — and most important of all — at that point it will be you alone, and not God, who will determine what is good and what is evil, what is right and what is wrong. No outside power will ever again be able to tell you what to do and what not to do. You yourself will determine your own behavior. "You will be as God, knowing good and evil." You need only break free from God's self-serving command and eat of the mysterious fruit. Once you do this, you will have autonomy over your own lives.

Autonomy: this is the delicious temptation that the serpent is offering to Eve. Autonomy of the self, independence from God, and, ultimately, rebellion against God's dominion. You will make your own determination of how to behave and how to live. You and no one else will make that decision.

Autonomy. Freedom. Independence: the prospects are irresistible. And so Eve, overcome by its limitless possibilities, tastes of the fruit, and she gives it to Adam to taste as well. And as the fruit becomes part of them, so does the overpowering desire to be autonomous become part of them, and part of mankind.

When Pharaoh asks, "Who is God that I should listen to His call?" he is expressing the desire for autonomy, independence, and rebellion that was implanted within mankind with the very first taste of that forbidden fruit.

Thus the battle lines are drawn: Pharaoh does not know who God is, does not recognize Him, and will not obey Him. The entire Exodus narrative, from the plagues to the crossing of the Red Sea, is a response to Pharaoh's question. The One God will see to it that Pharaoh finally recognizes Him.

Over and over again the theme is repeated:

> "Egypt shall know that I am God when I stretch forth My hand over Egypt and bring out the Children of Israel from their midst." (Exodus 7:15)

> "In order that you may know that there is none like the Lord our God." (ibid. 8:6)

> "That you may know that I am the Lord in the midst of the earth." (ibid. 8:18)

> "In order that you may know that to the Lord belongs the earth." (ibid. 9:19)

> "That you shall know that I am the Lord." (ibid. 10:2)

Pharaoh's theology is a uniquely contemporary concept: modern man is willing to believe in a Supreme Being and even to give Him obeisance — up to a point. That point is the red line which demarcates man's personal domain. Man is willing to listen to God's call as long as God does not cross that line and does not in any way impinge on man's personal freedom. That is to say: God can remain God, as long as he does not make any incursions into my autonomy, as long as he does not tell me how to live and what to do.

It is an eternal, unending struggle which pits man's desire to do as he pleases against God's command to do as God pleases and not as man pleases; man's insistence that he himself is sovereign, against God's insistence that there is an other beside man and an Other above man; man's conditional acceptance of God, versus God's demand that acceptance of Him means nothing unless it is unconditional.

Such is the nature of man: when one is filled with one's own self, there is no room for God to come in; when one empties himself of arrogance and pride, God is able to enter and to take his place within the heart.

Pharaoh lived almost four thousand years ago, but his words still resonate in many hearts. They do not accept the authority of any man or of any being. They are autonomous and, like gods, they claim the right to do as they please: "Who is God?"

Others identify with the words of Joseph. They understand their role in the universe, and God's role in the universe. They realize that man does have the powers of creation and destruction; that he can build up or tear down; that he can create life, and can bring on death; that man is but a little lower than the angels. But with all of these powers, they know that man is not God. They know that they are subservient to Him, and they are prepared to accept Him as their King:

"Am I in place of God?"

Two voices, two world views: *I am not God,* versus *I am god.* The future of each individual — as well as the future of all civilization — is determined by the choice of one view over the other.

12

And the Lord said:
I have seen
the affliction of My people in Egypt,
and heard its cry ....
I will send you unto Pharaoh,
that you may bring My people out of Egypt.
And Moses said to God:
Who am I,
that I should go to Pharaoh ....

Exodus 3:9-11

THE HUMILITY OF PRIDE:
WHO AM I?

At the burning bush, God orders Moses to go back to Egypt to bring His people out of slavery. Moses balks: *Mi anochi* — "Who am I to go to Pharaoh?" (Exodus 3:11).

On first reading, this is a statement of supreme humility: I am unworthy of this great task. But the phrase, "Who am I?" contains several levels of meaning beyond the obvious connotation of humility.

(Note, incidentally, that King David, when he is summoned to greatness, uses the identical words in II Samuel 7:18: *Mi anochi* — "Who am I?"

Similarly when King Saul, in I Samuel 18:18, proposes that David take the princess Merav, daughter of Saul, as a wife, David responds with the very same words: "Who am I...?")

In one sense, it can be read as a question of intense self-examination. Who am I really? What am I made of? All masks and disguises must now be removed. I must look at myself in the cold light of reality and uncompromising honesty. This is a question that reverberates down through the canyons of history, echoing and resounding.

Rebecca asks about Isaac: "Who is this man?"
(Genesis 24:65).
The blind and aged Isaac asks his son, "Who are you, my son?" (ibid. 27:18).
Before his death, Jacob asks about Joseph's sons, "Who are these?" (ibid. 48:8).
God asks Bilaam: "Who are these people?"
(Numbers 22:9).
Joshua asks the men of Gibeon: "Who are you?
(Joshua 9:8).
Saul asks twice about the young David: "Whose son is this lad?" (I Samuel 17: 56,58).
Saul asks the young Amalekite on the battlefield: "Who are you?" (ibid. 1:8).

The question cannot be evaded; it is heard throughout the Bible. And it is asked of each one of us as well. It demands that we face it, address it, and recognize its significance.

Who are you, and who am I? In my relationships — with others and with God — am I open or closed, generous or selfish, giving or taking, straightforward or devious? Am I kind and compassionate, or mean-spirited, cantankerous, and hard-hearted? Am I diligent or lazy, energetic or slothful? Is my life centered around the Me or around the You? Am I concerned about what I can do for others, or what others can do for me? Am I patient or impulsive? Am I honest with others? With myself? Am I an optimist or a pessimist? Am I able to give love and receive it? Do I harbor jealousy, resentment, hatred? Do I strive to understand people, or do I dislike people for no reason at all? Am I tolerant of my own errors, but supremely critical of the errors of others? Am I faithful or faithless? Do I truly trust in God? Do I reach out to Him in good times, or only in bad times? Do I strive to grow spiritually, or am I smug, self-satisfied, content with myself?

It is a painful exercise, this self-examination, but when it is done with integrity, we emerge from it cleansed and purified, ready to face the world — and our own selves. For self-knowledge is a formidable weapon in our struggle to become more human and more godly.

"Who am I?" also has a second connotation. It reminds us that we are not simply flesh and bones, but that we are God's handiwork. We bear within us a Divine soul. We are created from the earth, yes, but we are more than blobs of earth. We are, rather, creatures of God who have vast potential to wound, maim, and destroy — but we are created in the Divine image. In addition, we come from good stock: Abraham, Isaac, and Jacob are in our genes and are part of our soul. So much does our Creator have confidence in us that He entrusted us with His Torah, and placed us in charge of His world.

This reading of "Who am I?" is a source of pride in one's own potential and capacity for reaching great spiritual heights. Pride is not a negative quality in a person. Only false pride built on emptiness and vanity is destructive. But pride based on self-knowledge and on one's ultimate goals is a powerful force for spiritual growth and achievement.

Which flows into the third level of the question, "Who am I?" Literally, this is a statement of great humility: Who am I that I should be the one to take Israel out of Egypt? Choose someone else, someone more worthy.

For ordinary mortals the question resonates: Who am I to be deserving of God's beneficence? Who am I that God should give me so much goodness and so many gifts? I am unworthy, undeserving.

Humility, however, is not a simple matter. It is an important trait, but it must be handled with care. When humility obscures our potential for greatness, when it becomes a justification for lack of spiritual growth, when it descends into self-doubt and self-flagellation, humility can be a major negative force in life. It is not proud or arrogant to recognize that one has certain special qualities and skills and talents, as long as one also recognizes that these are Divine gifts, and that one must strive to be worthy of the One Above Who granted them. That is true humility.

Humility, in brief, is not a synonym for self-denigration. Moses, the most humble of all men, surely knew his qualities of greatness. But he also knew that whatever greatness he possessed was not of his own creation but was the gift of God. That he can twice say in all honesty to the rebellious Israelites (Exodus 16:7-8), *Venachnu mah* — "What are we?" — which implies that he and his brother Aaron are nothing and inconsequential — is not a contradiction to this sense of self-worth. Whatever he may seem to be — leader, prophet, visionary — is in essence nothing; whatever he is in essence is the gift of God.

Note that the Hebrew word for "humble" is *anav*. This is how the Torah describes Moses himself: "And the man Moses was extremely humble — *anav m'od* (Numbers 12:3). The Hebrew word for "humble" — *anav* — has its root in the word for "poor": *ani*. An *anav* is one who is poor in his own sight, who has no claims on anyone, who knows that without God he is nothing. It is the polar opposite of the person who is convinced that the world and all that is in it begins and ends with himself. It is this supreme quality of humility that connects Moses ineluctably with God, for in making himself as a thing of naught — not just an *anav*, but an *anav m'od* — he is in effect making God the Everything.

To be aware of one's strengths and one's potential and yet not become self-centered or arrogant — this is the secret of a Moses, the defining representation of true humility.

Can one be truly humble and at the same time be proud of one's origins and one's self? Yes. We have no less an example than that of the Creator Himself. For "R. Yochanan said, Wherever you find the greatness of the Holy One, Blessed Is He, there you find His humility." (Talmud, *Megillah*, 31a). He goes on to cite a number of Biblical references to God's majesty and His simultaneous humility, such as:

For the Lord your God is the God of gods and the Lord of Hosts, the great, mighty, and awesome God Who shows no regard for person and accepts no bribe" and immediately afterwards it says, "He upholds the cause of the fatherless and the widow, and loves the stranger, giving him food and clothing ...."

Hillel the Elder also provides a model. Hillel was known as the exemplar of a humility that rivaled that of Moses. When Hillel died he was eulogized as O *anav*, O *hasid* (devout one) ... (Jerusalem Talmud *Sotah* 9:13, 45b; see also *Shabbat* 31a). And yet it is Hillel who declares about himself, *Im ani kan, hakol kan* — "If I am here, everyone is here" (*Sukkah* 53a).

Similarly, the Mishnah (*Sanhedrin* 37a) refers to the singularity and significance of each individual on earth.

Whoever destroys a single soul of Israel, Scripture reckons it as if he destroyed an entire world, and whoever preserves a single soul of Israel, Scripture reckons it as if he had preserved an entire world ....

The Mishnaic text continues:

The Holy One Blessed Is He fashioned every man in the stamp of the first man, and yet none of them resembles his fellow. Therefore every single person must say: For my sake was the world created.

It is easy to distort humility. The Talmud (*Gittin* 56a) relates how the misplaced humility of one sage brought about the destruction of the Temple. The perils of misplaced humility are embodied in the words of the prophet Samuel to King Saul: "Although you are small in your own eyes, you are the head of the tribes of Israel, and God Himself anointed you as King over Israel" (I Samuel 15:17).

Mi anochi — "who am I?" That word, *anochi,* bears scrutiny. For consider: What is the very first word of the Ten Commandments? That same word: *Anochi:* "I am the Lord your God Who took you out of Egypt ...." *Anochi* here refers to God Himself.

Who, then, can say of himself that he is an *anochi,* when there is only a single *Anochi* in the universe? Only an arrogant Pharaoh, who is convinced that he himself is a god, does not ask, "Who am I," but asks instead, "Who is God?" He will brook no competition from others who claim his own authority. But for ordinary people, there is only one *Anochi* in the universe, the *Anochi* Who took us out of Egypt. Although we are created in His image, we are but miniature *anochi*'s, pale replicas of the One *Anochi.*

Once we know the response to that ultimate question — that there is only one genuine *Anochi* — all else falls easily into place. Once we recognize the One *Anochi,* then we can truly look at our selves, the creatures of that *Anochi,* and begin to understand true humility and true pride.

Who am I? I am nothing.
Who am I? I am everything.

13

And Moses said to the Lord:
Why have You brought evil upon this people?
Why have you sent me?
...You have not delivered the people ....

Exodus 5:22-23

THE MYSTERY IN THE CLEFT OF THE ROCK: WHY HAVE YOU BROUGHT EVIL UPON THIS PEOPLE?

At the burning bush, God calls upon Moses to assume the leadership of the children of Israel and to deliver them from the bondage of Egypt. Moses resists the call: "I beg of you, O God, find someone else; I am unworthy, not at all qualifed for this task; I have a speech defect; the people do not know me, they will not follow me; my older brother Aaron is far more worthy."

God will not be dissuaded, and before His insistent command, Moses finally has no choice but to accept. The mission is thrust upon him.

But with every demand that Moses makes of Pharaoh, the burden of the Children of Israel is intensified and their troubles increase. Now they are not even given straw to make bricks. The people cry out against Moses.

Moses turns to God: "You promised me that I would help deliver the people from their bondage. But since I began to intercede on their behalf, their situation has worsened." And Moses asks a terrible question of his Creator (Exodus 5:22)

Lamah harei-'ota la-'am ha-zeh? — "Why have You allowed so much evil to come upon this people ...." Why have you sent me? This is not how things were supposed to be. I expected matters to turn out differently. This is the very opposite of what You led me to believe.

Lamah: Why? The Hebrew word also means *l'mah,* for what purpose, for what reason? The question is defiant — it seems to point an accusing finger at God Himself — but it originates in the love of Moses for his people.

Moses is not the first to challenge God's justice. In fact, Moses echoes the very first challenge to God's justice that, centuries earlier, was uttered by Abraham concerning the inhabitants of Sodom (Genesis 18:23).

But the two challenges are not at all analogous. Abraham's earlier questions before God are not explosions of anger and bitterness. They are more negotiation than accusation. Abraham, of course, was concerned with what might appear as the injustice of God, and with the moral problem of innocents dying with the guilty — but in his dialogue with God he is much less pointed and direct. We do not hear Abraham declaring, "How can You, the Judge of all the earth, even contemplate such injustice?" Instead we hear him pleading, and we hear a genuine statement of wonder: "Will the Judge of all the earth not do justice?" That is inconceivable; obviously, the God of justice will act justly.

In contrast, the question of Moses is astonishing in its audacity and boldness — the more so because it is uttered by the same Moses whom the Torah itself characterizes as the most humble man on the face of the earth (Numbers 12:3). Moses here is not meek; he offers no apologies and genuflections as does Abraham, who keeps saying, *"Allow me one more question; do not be offended if I make one more request."*

The attitude of Abraham is one of a servant before his Master. The attitude of Moses — dare one even say it? — is the attitude of a prince before the King. Each one challenges God. But the one challenge is wrapped in velvet; the other challenge is unwrapped entirely, raw and harsh and bitter.

But our astonishment at Moses' language is mitigated by the special context in which he speaks, far different from the context of Abraham's discussion. Abraham's challenge is directed at an action that God is contemplating: His declared intention to destroy Sodom. Moses's challenge concerns what has already taken place: the worsening condition of his people. Abraham has not seen the destruction, for it has not yet occurred; he can feel no pain at something that might take place tomorrow; he simply tries to prevent that something from happening. Moses, however, has witnessed the worsening condition, has heard the cries, and has felt the pain.

Further, Abraham is dealing with an abstraction, a city whose people he does not know and with whom he has no relationship. Moses is referring to his own people, Israel, whom he has been sent to rescue, and this pain and anguish underlies his outburst.

(Later, in the Wilderness, Moses echoes his own words when, in deep despair at the bitter and unending complaints of the people, he asks God to relieve him of the burdens of leadership. Rarely in the entire Bible do we find words more searing and more affecting than this cri de coeur *— which also begins with that ubiquitous word, "lamah":*

Lamah hare-ota *— "Why have You done evil to Your servant"; why have I not found favor in Your eyes that You place the burden of this entire people upon me? Did I conceive this entire people or did I give birth to it, that You say to me, Carry them in your bosom as a nurse carries a suckling, to the Land that You swore to its forefathers? ... I alone cannot carry this* *entire nation, for it is too heavy for me. And if this is how You deal with me, then kill me now, if I have found favor in Your eyes, And let me not see my evil [Numbers 11:11-15].)*

The inner torment and anguish of Moses are almost palpable. But beyond the heartache and grief that generate these words, something quite illuminating emerges: only someone whose relationship with God is extremely intimate — like that of a child and a parent — could permit himself such an outburst of unadorned and naked honesty. Here we have the living manifestation of what God means when, in the very next chapter, He defines how Moses differs from all other prophets:

> *If there shall be among you prophets, in a vision shall I, God, make Myself known to him; in a dream shall I speak with him. Not so is My servant Moses; in My entire house he is the trusted one. Mouth to mouth do I speak to him, in clear vision and not in riddles; at the very image of God does he gaze ....*

Moses is a human being, born of a man and woman (Exodus 2:1-2). Like a human being, he is not immune to frustration, disappointment, or despair. But at the same time he towers like a majestic mountain over all other men in his close relationship to his Creator: "mouth to mouth do I speak to him, in clear vision ... at the very image of God does he gaze."

It is noteworthy that many years later, another leader of Israel asks a question remarkably similar to that first *lamah* of Moses. In Judges 6:13, Gideon is "beating out wheat in the wine-press to hide it from the Midianites. An angel of the Lord appeared unto him, and said: The Lord is with you, you mighty man of valor."

Gideon's response is swift and to the point: "Pardon, my lord, if the Lord be indeed with us, *lamah* — why — has all this befallen us? And where are all His wonders that our fathers have told us, saying, 'Did not the Lord bring us out of Egypt?' Now the Lord has forsaken us and delivered us into the hands of Midian."

Gideon's chilling words bear within them a bitter echo of the complaint of Moses. Both leaders share a burden of frustration and pain, and both are able to express their frustration in clear, unmistakable — and audacious — words.

And what is most striking is that the Divine Object of these challenges from His creatures does not react in anger, but with indulgence, forbearance, and understanding.

Man's questions about God's justice, about the meaning of evil and tragedy and suffering, reverberate down through the centuries. *Lamah?* Why, O God, must this sadness take place? To what end, to what purpose, is the death of this innocent child, the pain of that young mother, the anguish of this father and mother over their tragedy? I believe in You, I trust in You, I hope in You, but why this?

Lamah? It is more than a question; it is a howl of pain. Not only on a personal level: *lamah,* why must the Jewish people suffer, why must we be scorned, why must we and our Land be the object of such hatred?

King David in Psalm 77 expresses it in heartrending prose, also in the form of questions:

On the day of my distress I sought the Lord; in the night my hand was stretched out ... my soul refused to be comforted ....

> *Will the Lord cast me off forever?*
> *Will He nevermore give His favor again?*
> *Is His kindness spent forever?*
> *Is His promise come to an end for all generations?*
> *Has God forgotten to be gracious?*
> *Has He shut up His mercies in anger?*

Psalm 87:15, among many other psalms, expresses it in identical terms:

Lamah — "Why O Lord do You cast off my soul?"

In a word: *Lamah?* Why is there such an abundance of tears in the world? Surely You could have created a world of sunshine and fluffy white clouds and windless days and green grass and jolly roses and peace and love and laughter and the sounds of children playing.

Why have You allowed such evil to inhabit Your world? To what end, to what purpose? I know, my God, that there must be a purpose, I know there is an answer to my *Why*. I trust in You and I know that the universe is not barren and desolate. I know that You are present in all places and that You are the Guide and the Instrument. But you have created in me the desire to know why, to penetrate beneath the level of what is. There is an answer to my *Why*; somewhere there is a hint that begins with "because ...." I know that my mortal self is not able to comprehend the immortal and the eternal; that my ephemeral, transitory being cannot compprehend the ultimate "because." But if only I could perceive a tiny corner of the vast panorama that encompasses it, my anguish would be somewhat eased; if perhaps I could be granted a fleeting glimpse behind that impenetrable curtain, perhaps my pain would subside. And if I cannot know why I suffer, if I could at least know that I suffer for Your sake, that would, for now suffice.

Suffering and death are integral parts of the world, for reasons that are not discernible to the human mind. This I know and this I accept. But why must it be so? *Lamah?* I will never know the full answer to my *lamah*, but I will continue to ask it because to ask it, to be inquisitive, to strive for meaning and purpose, is an integral part of the Divine within me. I believe, I trust, but I must nevertheless ask, because not to ask and not to engage in the quest will render me less human.

The *lamah* resounds again in Exodus 32:12. After the sin of the Golden Calf, God declares His intention to destroy the people Israel. Moses responds with *lamah*: "Why does Your wrath burn against Your people …?" And in the very next verse Moses repeats the *lamah*: "Why should Egypt say, 'For evil purposes did He bring them out of Egypt'…." What Divine purpose will be served by destroying Your people? After all, You have promised their forefathers that You would bring their seed into the Land.

To this *lamah*, God responds positively: He rescinds His decree. And then Moses, attempting to open even wider the door leading to God's essence, makes this eternally haunting request: "Show me Your glory" (Exodus 33:18).

What did Moses mean? Say the Sages: He pleaded with God to reveal to him the answer to the eternal question that mocks and challenges the justice of God: why it is that the righteous suffer and the wicked prosper? When the righteous suffer and the evil prosper, that unsettles the delicate balance of the universe; it tarnishes, so to speak, the glory and the splendor of God. Once I understand this, says Moses, the full glory of God will be restored. Show me, therefore, Your glory, glistening and untarnished.

Moses is asking for no less than the answer to the ultimate *lamah*, the ultimate *Why*. In response, God instructs him to climb down into the cleft of the rock, because God's Presence is about to pass by. Moses descends into the cleft, awaiting God's answer. God covers the face of Moses with His Divine hand, as it were; God's Presence passes by; and then He proclaims that only that which is at the back of God can be seen by mortal man, "but My face will not be seen." Man might dimly perceive certain things, perhaps long after they have occurred, after God has passed by — but man will never understand fully and clearly the subtle ways of God or the labyrinthine byways of God's justice. Man, in sum, will never unlock the secret to the mystery. For, as the Psalmist phrases it, *mishpatecha tehom rabbah* — "Your judgments are like the great deep waters …" (Psalms 36:7).

Man will always be troubled by the same question: where is justice? And God will always provide the same answer: Descend into the cleft of the rock. Your question cannot be answered unless you lower yourself. Descend into the bedrock of existence, and only in that descent, only as you yourself become as one with the materials of creation itself, only as your mortal eyes are covered so that you know that you do not see, only then will you be able to discern My shadow as it passes you by. The answer to your terrible question, your legitimate and awe-filled question, cannot be understood if your eyes remain open and you stand tall and proud and erect upon the earth. But if you descend from yourself and lower yourself into the bowels of the rock of the earth — there, as you crouch down with your eyes covered, you might catch a fleeting glimpse of My mystery, and there the question that you place before Me will no longer demand a response from Me. Only down there, in the unyielding rock from which the universe was hewn, can you witness My Presence, and only there, stooped and bent over, can your anguished questions about My justice and My conduct of My universe begin to be asked.

14

Is there a lack of graves in Egypt
that you have taken us
to die in the wilderness.
What is this you have done to us,
to take us out of Egypt?

Exodus 14:11

DESPAIR AND BITTERNESS:
IS THERE A LACK
OF GRAVES IN EGYPT?

The utter bitterness of the sarcasm, and the burning anger at Moses, fairly leap from these words of the Jewish people. What motivates this outburst? The previous verse illuminates the source of the bitterness:

Pharaoh drew close: the children of Israel lifted up their eyes and behold, Egypt was pursuing them, and they feared greatly, and the children of Israel cried out unto the Lord (Exodus 14:10).

The onrushing Egyptians are closing in on them. In mortal fear, they turn to God in prayer. This much is understandable. What is not understandable is how it can be that in one moment they cry out to God for salvation, and in the very next breath they lash out in such fury against their earthly leader?

It is fear that motivates the prayer. Is it the same fear that motivates the fury against Moses? Do they feel that he is an impostor, that he is not in fact fulfilling the will of God in taking them out of Egypt? Have they lost all faith and trust in him as their leader? We cannot suggest that this is merely a temporary aberration, a panic and hysteria brought on by the sight of the pursuing Egyptians, because, as we will see below, the Israelites repeatedly complain against the leadership of Moses.

It is a difficult question. There is a dissonance between the prayer to God and the attack on Moses. Something seems to be missing in the sequence of events.

Ramban, echoing *Mechilta Beshalach* (§2), suggests that this is not a contradiction: among the Children of Israel were different sectors and groups, each with its own agenda. Some prayed, but others attacked Moses' leadership. Those who cried out to God did not attack Moses; those who attacked Moses did not cry out to God. It was truly a "mixed multitude" that left Egypt. That Moses was able to exercise authority over them is a testimony to the Divine gift of leadership that was granted him.

This is not the only time we witness such an outburst. In Exodus 15:24, at the Marah encampment, the Israelites complain to Moses about the lack of water: "What shall we drink?" This is at least a straightforward complaint, unaccompanied by invective and bitterness.

When they arrive at the Wilderness of Sin, there is further complaining:

If only we had died by the hand of God in the land of Egypt, where we sat by the fleshpots, when we ate bread to satiety — for you have taken us out to this Wilderness to kill this entire congregation by famine (Exodus 16:3).

Here we see how the complainers, blinded by their present fury, actually imagine their tenure in Egypt to have been not one of servitude and unremitting slavery, but a pleasant interlude that included pots of delicious meat and satisfying bread.

This, incidentally, is the only time that a direct question is not asked — although the Hebrew for "if only we had died" (mi yiten muteinu) does contain interrogative elements.

Questions are often answered with other questions. In response to all the complaining, God has His own question to the Israelites: "How long will you refuse to observe My commandments and My teachings?" (ibid. 16:28)

In Exodus 17, at the Rephidim encampment, there is again a lack of water, and again we find an angry question: "The people thirsted there for water, and the people complained against Moses, [this time more bitterly]: 'Why have you brought us up from Egypt to kill me and my children and my livestock through thirst?'" (ibid. 17:3). Moses fully senses their rage, and cries out to God: "A bit more and they will stone me."

It is not only the lack of water about which they complain. They also miss their meat.

The mixed multitude cultivated a craving, and the Children of Israel wept again and said: "Who shall give us meat to eat? We remember the fish that we ate in Egypt for nothing; the cucumbers, the melons and the leeks and the onions and the garlic, but now our soul is dried away, there is nothing at all beside this manna before our eyes (Numbers 11:4-6).

Meat and melons and leek were hardly the normal menu for slaves in Egypt who were even denied basic straw with which to make bricks, but such is the distorting power of discontent. Later, for example, Dathan and Abiram, leaders of the Korach rebellion against Moses, refer to Egypt, the land of their enslavement, as — astonishingly — "a land flowing with milk and honey" (ibid. 16:13)!

In Numbers 14:2, after the negative report of the spies, the Israelites again murmur against their leadership, this time because of the fear of entering Canaan. And once again, we hear questions:

If only we had died in the land of Egypt, or if only we had died in this wilderness. Why has the Lord brought us to this land, to fall by the sword, that our wives and children should be a prey? Were it not better for us to return to Egypt?

Note that here it is not Moses who is the object of their complaint, but God Himself.

The perennial complaints about water continue to surface. Miriam dies as Israel enters the Wilderness of Zin, and their miraculous supply of water dries up (no coincidence, since the waters in the desert, according to *Taanit* 9a, were in the merit of Miriam, who had waited for the infant Moses at the edge of the waters). Once again they quarrel with Moses, and once again we hear a tormenting question:

If only we had died as our brethren died before God. Why have you brought the congregation of God to this wilderness to die there, we and our animals? And why did you bring us out of Egypt to this evil place — not a place of seeds or fig, or grape, or pomegranate; and there is no water to drink (Numbers 20:3-5).

Here the Egyptian slave menu is expanded to sumptuous meals that include not only meat and onions, but also figs, grapes, and pomegranates: again discontent leads to a rage that distorts reality and creates a desert mirage.

A short time later, the Israelites are forced to make a detour around the land of Edom, which had refused them passage rights. Once again, in almost the same phrases, they cry out:

Why did you bring us up from Egypt to die in this Wilderness? For there is no food and no water, and [referring to God's gift of the manna] our soul is disgusted with this miserable bread" (ibid. 21:5).

More rage-induced distortion: even the manna's miraculous properties are "disgusting" and "miserable."

What is noteworthy about the complaints against Moses is that only in the first one — in Exodus 14 — is the complaint accompanied by a prayer to God. After that, we find no prayer at all. If, as Ramban suggests, there were in fact different sects among the Jews, and some of them prayed to God and did not murmur against their leadership, the praying ones seem to have grown completely silent through the rest of the sojourn in the wilderness.

Note also that, in all but one instance, the complaints are couched in the form of taunting questions. (Once again we encounter the rhetorical power of a question as opposed to a mere accusation.)

It is no wonder that Moses asked God to be relieved of his leadership — once again the form of a question: "How can I myself alone bear your care and your [Israel's] burden and your strife?" (Deuteronomy 1:12). And at the end of his life, he reminds his people of their abominable behavior:

> *Remember, do not forget, how you provoked the Lord your God to anger in the wilderness; from the day that you did depart from the land of Egypt until you came to this place, you have been rebellious against the Lord (ibid. 9:7).*

Complaining, whining, bemoaning, lamenting, murmuring, grumbling, yearning for the good old days — it is small wonder that Moses, in his farewell address to Israel, admonishes them: "Rebellious have you been against the Lord from the day I have known you" (ibid. 9:24).

Perhaps the cause of this schizophrenic behavior of the people — acutely aware of God's Presence and yet apparently ungrateful to Him and to Moses — is that they had lost sight of who they were, where they came from, and where they were going. They were the nation of Israel, the offspring of the Patriarchs, the bearers of God's mission on earth. When these are forgotten, the spiritual components within man drain away, and the physical rises to the top of the consciousness. Thus, despite their exposure to the reality of God, they revert time and again to the primordial concerns of their appetites and earthly needs. Quickly they forget the miracles that encompass them — their departure from Egypt, the splitting of the Sea, the Revelation of God at Sinai. The glorious past is gone, and the promise of the future — the Land of Promise, the eternal protection of the Almighty — means nothing to them. Their bodies and their physical needs overpower all else. All that matters to them is the now, the present. And once the emphasis is on the physical now, there can be no satisfaction, for there is always the need for more, and there is always some reason to bemoan and lament the present condition.

Once one embarks on the road of complaints, there are very few exits. The complaint soon engenders a whine, and then a lament, and then frenzied imagination takes over, all contact is lost with reality, the delicious and satisfying manna that falls daily from heaven is detested, and, in the fog of discontent, even slavery is confused with lavish feasts of meat and leeks and melons.

The Generation of the Wilderness experienced the very manifestation of God, and yet seemed completely unaware of His Presence in their midst. Their self-engendered discontent created within them envy, heartache, and never-ending bitterness. They are a living negative reminder of what the Sages were to stress many years later in Avot 4:1: "Who is wealthy? [again a question!] He who is satisfied with his lot." God Himself can be standing beside us, but if we are dissatisfied with our lot, we grow blind to His Presence and we see only our own selves and our own needs.

It is not an easy task to transform this principle from theory to reality, but the bitter barbs that the Israelites hurled against the man who liberated them serve as a sobering reminder of what can occur even to the most spiritual of people if they do not strive constantly to transcend the physical and to give primacy to higher things.

This is not the place for self-help advice on how to handle anger and bitterness, but on a national, Jewish-people level, a useful beginning step is to reverse what the Israelites did: to focus on who we are (creatures of God); to recall our origins (a long line of Jews who have remained loyal to Him despite many temptations to abandon Him); and to remember where we are going (to continue witnessing to the world that there is a God above). Those who bear in mind these eternal Jewish truths will inevitably find its refraction in their personal lives as well. The knowledge that we are all Divine creatures beloved and cherished by God, and that each individual is an integral part of His plan for the world, shields us from sinking into the trough of chronic dissatisfaction, and offers us a new sense of pride in self, a genuine joy and contentment that we have been chosen to be an integral part of this ancient people, Israel.

The despair and the bitterness of the two terrible Biblical questions — "Is there a lack of graves in Egypt?" and "Were it not better for us to return to Egypt?" — can be transformed into something positive if two other Biblical questions are allowed to serve as a counterweight: "Who are you, my son?" (Genesis 27:18) — which looks inward at the potential greatness of each individual creature of God; and "What do you seek?" (ibid. 37:15) — which looks outward at the possibilities of a future marked by genuine seeking.

15

If you see the donkey of your enemy
lying under its burden
and you would forbear from helping him,
you must surely help him.

Exodus 23:5

THE UNADORNED YOU:
WOULD YOU
NOT HELP YOUR ENEMY?

Exodus 23:5 states: "If you see the donkey of your enemy lying under its burden" — *v'chadalta me'azov lo, 'azov ta'azov imo* .... The literal translation would be: "... and you would forbear from helping him; you must surely help him." That is to say, even though your natural impulse would be not to help your enemy, nevertheless, you are obligated to help him.

This is an apparently straightforward commandment instructing us to help another person in distress, even if he is an enemy. But the reading of Rashi, while maintaining the same meaning, is not so straightforward, and transforms the verse into a profound insight into human nature.

Rashi suggests that we read the middle phrase *bitmiyah*, as if it were an incredulous question: "... would you forbear from helping him?" That is to say: surely you, a human being with a heart and with sensitivity, would not forbear from helping a fellow human being in distress, even though he is your enemy. Continues the text: 'azov ta'azov imo — which can be read not only as a commandment — "you will surely help him" — but also as a goad and a prod: "surely you will help him."

The Torah in this verse does not simply direct us to help a person in distress, as it does in Deuteronomy 2:4: "You shall not see your brother's donkey or his ox fall down by the way and hide yourself from them; you shall surely help him to lift them up." In our Exodus text, the Torah goes further: you must help that other person even if he is your enemy. And in our text the Torah does not merely utter a command, but instead issues the command in the form of a question — a question designed to bring us up short and to reveal the inner decency and instinctive humanity that resides within each one of us. Is it conceivable that you would continue on your way and not lend a helping hand to this man — even though he is your enemy? Surely you will help him — for two reasons: a) I command you to do so; and b) your better nature within you also commands you to do so.

By formulating the directive as a question, the Torah appeals to my deeper instincts to do good, to be of help, to lend a hand. It taps me gently on the shoulder and reminds me of what is expected of me as a human being.

To read this as a question is startling because of its extraordinary expectations of human nature. Consider the scenario: I am on my donkey, traveling from one village to another. There on the path in front of me I encounter my sworn enemy standing forlorn beside his donkey. The poor beast has collapsed under its heavy load. It is sprawled out on the ground, unable to rise up, unable to go on. My enemy tries to lift the donkey and his burden, but he cannot do it alone. He needs help. First he must unload everything so that the donkey can stand on its feet, and then he must reload it once again onto the donkey's back.

I feel sorry for the beast, but I do not feel sorry for my enemy. My natural, all too human inclination is to smile at the just retribution that has been meted out to my enemy, and to continue blithely along my way. That I should interrupt my journey and dismount from my own animal and help my enemy to reload his donkey — this does not occur to me; it does not even enter my consciousness. This kind of forgiving goodness, this overlooking of past wrongs, is something that cannot be expected of a normal human being with normal human reactions. This man is my enemy because of certain things he has done to me: he has wronged me, gossiped about me, hurt me, destroyed my property, stolen from me. He hates me, and I hate him in return. To the Torah's question, "Would you forbear from helping him?" my immediate, instinctive answer would be a resounding "Yes, I would — and should — forbear." The last thing in the world that I would want to do is to help this enemy in his time of need.

The Torah, however, expects us — in fact, demands of us — to go beyond our natural human instincts. It expects us to transcend the urge to hurt or maim when we are angry; to overcome illicit desires when we are under strong temptation; to override the instinct to focus only on the self and instead to focus on the other through *chesed* and *tzedakah*.

Similarly, it expects us not to take revenge on those who have wronged us. My neighbor, for example, wants to borrow my shovel. Last month, when I wanted to borrow his hammer, he refused me. I am now tempted to behave in kind and to refuse him just as he refused me. But the Torah expects otherwise of me: *Lo tikom* — "you shall not take revenge" (Leviticus 19:18). Yes, it is perfectly natural to want to take revenge, but God wants us to be able to transcend the ordinary and the merely instinctive and natural.

It is also likely that by commanding me to help my enemy, the Torah has a larger design in mind: the reduction and ultimate elimination of the enmity between us. For can it be possible — after I help my enemy re-load his donkey, and after we lift together, and push together, and grunt together, and sweat together — that he and I can still harbor the same ill-will for one another as we did before I dismounted my beast to help him?

Perhaps this is the backdrop to the reading of Rashi. All of the Torah is designed to move us out of the orbit of self-centeredness, away from the focus on the Me. Here we have an opportunity to demonstrate that we have successfully internalized the teachings of the Torah and that we are able to move beyond impulse and instinct onto a higher human plane. *Would you not help this person who is in trouble, even though he is your enemy? Of course you would help him, because you are a person who lives by the law of God and the law of His Torah.*

How much more suggestive is this reading of Rashi than the obvious reading that takes it merely as a declarative sentence. The commandment as a question reflects a Torah that expects of its adherents a level of behavior that transcends the natural human reactions. To behave super-naturally, to transcend our instincts: this is what is to be the standard of behavior. For the Jew of Torah, it is expected that the extraordinary becomes ordinary.

It is only fair that this be so. After all, we expect our Creator to behave towards us in an extraordinary way, do we not? We sin, transgress, violate His laws in a hundred different ways; we forget His teachings, we overlook, disregard, rationalize. And each time we ask Him to disregard our failings, to forgive us our sins, to wipe away our transgressions, to remember that we are only flesh and blood, to overlook the fact that we have overlooked. We beg Him to treat us with patience, understanding, forbearance. As the Psalmist puts it in 130:3, *Im avonot tishmar Y-ah, HaShem, mi ya'amod* — "if Thou, God were to preserve iniquities, O Lord, who could stand?"

What we expect of our Creator, our Creator in turn expects of us. The question gives us pause: would you desist from helping this person just because he is your enemy? Surely you would not withhold help from him when he is in distress. Surely you would not permit your natural impulse for satisfaction at his distress to dominate your reaction. As a faithful Jew, you know that you are expected to override the merely instinctive and the merely impulsive. You will realize that your enemy is also a human being, and, seeing his distress, you will set aside the animal instinct within you and you will behave as a Godly human being.

And when at last we painfully but successfully fulfill this most difficult commandment, then we can turn to God and pray that He, too, will treat us, His erring and willful children, with the same forbearance and understanding.

Would You, O God of mercy and compassion and love, refrain from helping us in our distress just because we have strayed from Your path?

16

What does the Lord ask of you.?

Deuteronomy 10:12

What does the Lord require of you...?

Micah 6:8

 ## THE BOTTOM-LINE ESSENTIALS: *WHAT DOES THE LORD REQUIRE OF YOU...?*

Two prophets, two questions to Israel. The first is from Moses:

What does the Lord your God ask (sho'el) of you but (ki-im) to fear the Lord your God, to walk in His ways, and to love Him, and to serve the Lord your God with all your heart and with all your soul, to keep the commandments of the Lord and His statutes which I command you this day for your good (Deuteronomy 10:12).

The second is from Micah:

What does the Lord require (doresh) of you, but [again the words ki-im] doing justice, loving kindness, and walking humbly with your God? (Micah 6:8)

Let us examine Micah first. On the face of it he, like Moses, is making a very modest demand of Israel. This impression is under-scored by the manner in which the demand is phrased. Micah's question, like that of Moses, reads as if it were a very simple request. In effect, he seems to be saying this: God's command-ments may appear to be complex and difficult, but the fact is that God requires only the following three things from you. This is the clear implication of the *ki-im* — "*but*" or "*only*": God, after all is said and done, requires very little of us, only three slight duties.

Upon a closer look, however, the demand is not so slight, nor is it easily understood or implemented. Look, for example, at the first requirement: *asot mishpat* — "do justice." What exactly is justice? Who defines it? And how does one go about "doing" it?

As for the second — *ahavat chesed* — "loving kindness": of course we love mercy and kindness. Who would not? But that, too, upon examination presents some questions. What is kindness, and what does "loving" it really entail? Is there a difference between lov-ing kindness and doing kindness? Is it enough to love kindness in the abstract without actually performing acts of kindness? And, once again, what precisely is the meaning of that word *chesed*, which we translate as "mercy" or "lovingkindness"?

Why, incidentally, are we asked to *do* justice, but to *love* mercy? Can we not do kindness and love justice?

Perhaps Micah is suggesting that the essence of true kindness is love from within and not merely action from without. Obviously, kindness must be done and not remain within the recesses of the human heart. Unless it is acted upon, it remains a hollow sentiment with little or no effect on anyone else. But genuine mercy, the kind God wants us to have, is not the external act of kindness alone, but an act that emanates from within. Justice, on the other hand, must be meted out without recourse to emotions; one does justice, and acts it out physically. Justice stems from the intellect. By utilizing judgment and knowledge, by thinking and considering and weigh-ing alternative resolutions to an issue, one can arrive at a judgment that will be just.

Kindness, in a word, is based on emotion, feeling, and love that translate into the act of mercy. Justice is quite independent of inner feelings. It is based on evidence, witnesses, cool logic, and reason — all of which translate into the act of justice. It is not enough to love justice; one must implement it. It is not enough to do kindness; it must well up from within.

The third demand — *hatzne'a lechet* — walking humbly with your God — adds to the ambiguity. That one should be humble and should believe in God seems eminently reasonable, but the demand is greater than that. We must walk humbly with God. Perhaps it means that whatever one does religiously should be done in a humble way, and that service of God should be performed quietly, without fanfare and noise. That, too, is a lovely sentiment — but are there not times when God should be served with pride and with openness? And why walk humbly only with God? Should we not walk humbly with our fellow human beings as well? As the words sink in, the questions intensify. How does one define "humble"? And that word *walking* — just what is the meaning of "walking with God"?

A more significant issue: the implication is that if one fulfills these three requirements, the Lord requires nothing else. If so, what about the six hundred and thirteen commandments of the Torah? Does the performance of these three demands absolve one from observing the other mitzvot of the Torah?

Micah's words echo those of Moses in the Torah, but his words are not identical to those of Moses. Micah's question is much more succinct, compressing the thirty-one-word demand of Moses into his own ten words — but the formulation of the question is the same. The key to the similarity is the common usage of the *ki-im* formula, meaning "merely" or "only," by both prophets.

Does Micah's one sentence encapsulate all that Moses said?

Not quite. For one thing, Moses uses the word *sho'el*, which means "ask," while Micah uses *doresh*, which means "seek," or "demand," or "require." The two Hebrew verbs are similar to one another, but *doresh* appears to be the stronger term. So while

Micah makes only three demands, they are demands and not simply requests. Moses, on the other hand, lists six: 1) to fear God; 2) to walk in His ways; 3) to love God; 4) to serve God unreservedly; 5) to keep His mitzvot; 6) to keep His statutes. Only some of these can be subsumed under Micah's three demands. Micah seems to ignore the others.

But even though Moses uses the more muted *sho'el*, he makes it very clear and unambiguous that the commandments of the Torah are central ("keep the mitzvot and statutes"). While Moses begins with apparently ambiguous demands like fearing and loving God and walking in His ways, he ends with a call to observe all the commandments of the entire Torah.

Moses is not offering any easy prescriptions. He opens with "the Lord only asks," but he ends by saying that what the Lord wants from us is to observe everything. By contrast, Micah does not directly mention the mitzvot as such, but only alludes to them peripherally with his "walking with God."

There is another apparent difference. Moses seems to place equal emphasis on the relationships between man and God, and between man and man. But Micah, on the face of it, seems to place two-thirds of his emphasis on man-to-man (do justice; love mercy) but only one-third on man-to-God (walk humbly with your God). The Talmud proceeds to reduce even this one-third, stating that we walk humbly with God when we accompany the dead to burial, and when we assist brides (*Makkot* 24a). These are examples of man-to-man relationships, and thus the Talmud seems to be suggesting that this third requirement also deals with interpersonal matters, as well as with our relationship with God. Is Micah, then, relegating man-God obligations to a secondary position?

We raise more questions here than can be answered in this short space, but I would suggest that the differences between the presentations of Moses and Micah are only surface differences. Micah is certainly not devaluing the man-God interaction, nor is he overlooking the need to perform the mitzvot of the entire Torah. He is, rather, attempting to distill the essence of the Torah into one

sentence, and is saying that even as we observe all the commandments, we must always bear in mind those things that are often
taken for granted and therefore neglected: the doing of justice, the
loving of mercy, the walking through life with the humble awareness that God is present. That is to say, whatever mitzvot are
performed by us, hovering over them all should be justice, mercy,
and the Presence of God.

The Talmud notes the curious phrasing that Moses uses, a
phrasing that applies to Micah as well. In using the term *ki-im*
("only"), Moses implies that he is asking very little. The Sages are
curious (*Berachot* 33b; *Megillah* 25a): All these behaviors that
Moses requires — are they merely an "only"? "Is fear of God a
milta zutrata — a small matter?"

In truth, reply the Sages, "For someone like Moses it is in fact
a small thing." But who can presume to be a Moses? Even for the
Jew who is not a Moses, but observes the Torah, the rewards in
terms of satisfaction, serenity, and attitude make it all worthwhile,
and not as difficult as it may appear from the outside. For such a
Jew, the commandments are not harsh or burdensome. Instead,
they are viewed as guidelines and directives that are happily and
gratefully followed, knowing that the only other alternative is
chaos. He who observes the commandments cannot imagine living
in any other way. For such a person, non-observance of the Torah
would be a much heavier burden.

For those who do not observe the Torah, however, for those
who are on the outside looking in, the regimen does seem
extremely difficult. Perhaps Moses and Micah are attempting to
reassure those who are fearful that what appears to be a burdensome way of life can in fact become a fulfilling experience, and not
at all painful or forbidding. It is possible to live so and to become so
attached to God that the adherence to His commandments
becomes quite normal and natural — like breathing.

For example, the act of breathing in and out is a complicated procedure, and without it life cannot be sustained. And yet it is the most natural of human functions. So it is with the spiritual life. Its pinnacle is attained when one discovers that serving God is the most natural way to go through life. Moses and Micah promise us that some day — if we follow the commandments faithfully and adhere to God's teachings lovingly — the service of God can in fact become a *ki-im*, a "merely" and an "only," as natural as breathing. But one must make a beginning; one cannot remain on the sidelines, just as one cannot learn to swim if he remains on dry land.

By invoking the vivid image of walking, both Moses and Micah suggest that the religious life is not static, but involves a step-by-step approach towards our Creator. Their use of the root *holekh* — "walk" — prefigures the word *halakhah*, the term for Jewish law that projects the process of walking — towards God. The steps may be faltering ones, we might occasionally trip or stumble, but God helps us pick ourselves up and continue walking towards Him. In the journey towards closeness to Him, in the performance of the commandments, the bedrock ideas of Moses and Micah help energize our steps.

Thus, the daily challenge for each man and woman is to bring to life these demands: to act justly and mercifully in every encounter; to be aware with awe that there is a God above us; by means of the mitzvot, to move forward each day ("walk") towards His Presence, and not to remain static and immobile; and as we grow and develop and make progress, to do so knowing that God is the Master of all, and that He — and not we — is the final authority and arbiter in our lives.

Then we can become like Moses and like Micah: someone for whom the service of God and the service of man are spontaneous, artless, unpretentious, natural — a condition in which we will fear Him and love Him, do lovingkindness, perform His commandments, walk in His ways, deal justly and lovingly with everyone we encounter on our path, and remain humble before His Presence.

This is what the Lord seeks, requires, asks, and demands of us. From a distance, it is an insurmountable mountain climb. But once we embark on our upward trek, we discover with exhilaration that every day brings us closer and closer to the summit

A statement made by King David complements the ideas of Moses and Micah.

In Psalm 34:13-15, David asks a question similar to that of the two great prophets:

> *Mi ha-ish he-chafetz chaim...*
> *Who is the man who desires life,*
> *loves many days that he may see good?*
> *Guard your tongue from evil,*
> *and your lips from speaking guile.*
> *Turn away from evil and do good,*
> *seek peace and pursue it.*

Here we have another distillation of the quintessentials of the religious life, similar to the distillations of Moses and Micah. Like them, David introduces his essence in the form of a question, and like them, he responds with a concise definition.

But the similarities stop here. Unlike the responses of Moses and Micah, David's does not impose demands that God makes on us. Instead, we have a definition that points to our own self-interest.

Moses and Micah — beyond the suggestion that God's ways are not beyond man's capacity, and that they are eminently doable — offer no rewards, no inducements, and no benefits. They simply state that this is what God demands of you.

David, on the other hand, offers a formula for a full and rich life. Do you desire all the good that life has to offer? Then live in the following way.

On the face of it, the formula is quite simple: Speak no evil; be not deceitful; do good and not evil; and seek peace. This is certainly a fair bargain. In return for watching what I say and doing good and being peaceful, I receive in exchange a long life filled with good.

As was the case with Moses and Micah, there is more here than meets the eye.

David uses several words here that on their own are ambiguous and vague, and call out for greater sharpening. Key words such as "evil" — *ra* and "good" — *tov* are in fact used twice. It is as if we are being told that in order to see good, we must do good and stay away from evil.

The Biblical commentators offer a deeper understanding. For Ibn Ezra, the term "evil" refers to the "thou-shalt-not's" of the Torah; the term "good" refers to the "thou-shalt's." Thus, David is saying: if you desire the good life, do what the Torah commands and avoid what the Torah forbids. In a few words, David is encapsulating the requirement to follow the Torah as the guarantor of a good life.

Other commentaries expand on this: the word *tov* — "good" — is in itself another term for Torah. Thus, if you want to see *tov* — "good" — then live by *tov*, which is the Torah. Still others suggest that "life" does not refer simply to life on earth, but to eternal life. Thus, to live by Torah laws is to guarantee eternal life. (*Metzudat David*) Similarly, some readings offer the word *Shalom* — "peace" — as another name for God Himself: "Seek God; and even if He is not easily found, pursue Him."

In this Psalm, David echoes a question that he asks in Psalm 15: "O Lord, who shall abide in Your tent, who shall dwell in Your holy mountain?" In response, David lists eleven qualities:

He who walks uprightly,
and acts justly,
and speaks truth in his heart.
He who does not slander with his tongue,
nor does evil to his fellow,

nor takes up a reproach against his neighbor.
In whose eyes a vile person is despised,
but he honors them that fear the Lord.
He that swears to his own hurt and changes not.
He who puts not out his money on interest,
nor takes a bribe against the innocent.

The tendency to compress the six hundred and thirteen commandments of the Torah into a smaller package is endemic to classical Judaism. Thus we have R. Akiva's famous dictum that "love thy neighbor as thyself" (Leviticus 19:18) is the major principle of the Torah" (*Torat Kohanim* 19:45). And the great sage, Hillel, informs the would-be convert that the major teaching of Torah is this: "What is hateful to you, do not do to your friend: this is the entire Torah. The rest is commentary; go and learn it." (*Shabbat* 31a).

The Talmud itself refers to this phenomenon of encapsulization. After stating that the Torah contains six hundred and thirteen commandments — three hundred and sixty-five negative commandments and two hundred and forty-eight positive commandments — the Talmud (*Makkot* 24a) states that "David came and established them (*he'emidan*, lit., "stood them") on eleven," and goes on to cite the above Psalm 15.

Continues the Talmud:

Then came Isaiah and established them on six [principles], as in 33:15, where he asks, "Who among us shall dwell with the fire...?" [Fire is often synonymous with the word of God, and also with God Himself: cf Jerermiah 33:29, and Talmud Sheqalim 16b].

Continues Isaiah:

He that walks righteously and speaks uprightly; he that despises the gain of oppressions, that shakes his hand from holding of bribes, that stops his ears from hearing of blood, and shuts his eyes from seeing evil; he shall dwell on high." Then came Micah and established them on three [principles]: "to do justice, love mercy, and walk humbly with your God...." Isaiah came back and established them on two: "Keep judgment and do justice" (Isaiah 56:1). Came Amos and established them on one: "Thus says the Lord: Seek Me and live" (Amos 5:6). Came Habakkuk and established them on one: "[T]he righteous one shall live by his faith" (Habakkuk 2:4).

These attempts to compress the six hundred and thirteen commandments into eleven, or six, or three, or one overriding principles raise certain questions. Why this exercise? What about the balance of the Torah's commandments? If the entire Torah is found in a few general principles, then what of the other six hundred plus commandments? Is it being suggested that they are now unimportant, unnecessary, irrelevant?

Rashi in his commentary on the above Talmudic text, (s.v. "V'he-'emidan") writes:

Because in the beginning they were righteous and were capable of accepting the yoke of many commandments; but later generations were not so righteous, and if they attempted to observe all of them, there would be no one worthy of doing so. "So David came and established them on eleven..." so that they would be found worthy if they observed these eleven; and so it was constantly: the later generations reduced it [the Torah's commandments].

Rashi's commentary raises new questions, which are addressed by Maharsha (R. Shelomo Eidles, Poland, 1555–1632). Citing various classical authorities, Maharsha demonstrates that wherever we find cases of concision and compression, they are not exclusionary; that is, the intention is to subsume the entire range of commandments under the rubric of a broad, all-inclusive principle. Thus

Habakkuk's single principle, "the righteous shall live by his faith," signifies the faith in the first commandment, "I am the Lord your God," and in his very ambiguity Habakkuk encompasses the belief in God as the Giver of the Torah and faith in the Torah as God's revealed word at Sinai. All are subsumed under his one broad definition. Similarly, all the reductions cited by the Talmud contain in them practices that represent and include the entire range of Torah.

This may explain the unusual wording of the Talmud in *Makkot* 24. It does not state that David or Isaiah or Micah or Amos or Habakkuk "reduced" or "compressed" or "abbreviated" the Torah to these few principles. Rather, the word it uses is *he'emidan*, from the word *omed* — "*stand.*" Thus the proper meaning of the Talmudic phrase is that these prophets and teachers of Israel took the six hundred and thirteen commandments and "stood them," or "established them," or "placed them" on a foundation consisting of a few principles. These principles are not substitutes for the Torah. On the contrary, they embody and enclose within them all of the Torah. They form the tiny nucleus which ultimately expands into the entire range of Torah, the hidden bedrock from which the entire Torah is hewn, the linchpin that, though often overlooked, holds all the various commandments together. (The same can be said of the concise statement of Moses that we have already examined.)

These, then, are not diminutions of Torah; instead, they are an effort to capture its essence — just as Moses attempts to capture the elusive essence of God Himself when he asks Him: "Show me Your ways" (Exodus 33:13).

What does the Lord require, ask, demand of you?

Moses, Isaiah, Micah, Amos, Habakkuk, R. Akiva, Hillel would all agree: Be not apprehensive about the length of the journey. Start walking. Be not frightened by the task ahead, by the vast corpus of requirements and laws and practices and observances. Begin only with the tiny seed of a mitzvah genuinely performed, cultivate it faithfully, and tend it carefully, and before very long that seed will begin to develop into a giant oak tree resplendent with the full foliage of Torah and mitzvot.

17

I remember what Amalek did to Israel,
how he laid wait for him on the way,
when he came up from Egypt ….
Go and smite Amalek and utterly destroy
all that they have.
Have no mercy on them …
Oxen and sheep ….

I Samuel 15:2-3

The Sadness of King Saul: What is This Bleating of the Sheep in My Ears?

Prior to the battle with Amalek, the arch-enemy of Israel, the prophet Samuel gives his charge to Saul in the name of the Lord. Amalek must be utterly destroyed.

Saul wins the historic battle, and chapter 15, verse 8 in I Samuel, recounts his capture of Agag, king of Amalek. Verse 9 is the key: "And Saul and the people took pity on Agag and the best of the sheep …" and did not destroy them.

Saul returns in triumph. Flush with his victory, he informs the prophet Samuel that he has fulfilled God's command to wipe out Amalek and all its possessions. Samuel replies with a simple question: "And what is this bleating of the sheep that I hear …?" (I Samuel 15:14)

When Samuel had relayed God's command to Saul to kill Agag and to blot out Amalek, he added three apparently superfluous words: *velo tachmol alav* — "and have no pity on him" (ibid. 15:3). It is not clear if the warning against pity are the words of God that Samuel is relaying to Saul, or if they are an interpolation by Samuel himself who knows the heart of Saul and wishes to stiffen the king's resolve so that he not permit his own innate softness to interfere with the complete fulfillment of God's command. In any case, Saul has specifically been warned about taking pity: *velo tachmol.* In verse 9, after the conquest of Amalek, the text uses the very same word to point an accusatory finger at Saul: "But Saul and the people had pity — *vayachmol* — on Agag and on the best of the sheep ... and would not utterly destroy them."

God reacts swiftly, and informs Samuel that Saul has violated the Divine commandment. Samuel arises early to meet Saul, at which time Saul unabashedly declares that "I have performed the commandment of the Lord."

This is an astounding statement. Does not Saul know that he has done just the opposite? Surely Saul would not try to deceive the prophet of God.

No, Saul would not try to deceive Samuel; but he obviously believes that he has fully performed the commandment of the Lord. As for the fact that he has not actually destroyed all of Amalek, including its king and its livestock — that, Saul is certain, can be easily explained.

It is here that Samuel, in verse 14, asks his terrifying question — a question that must penetrate to the core of Saul and in fact reverberates down through the centuries as a challenge to all who would blithely explain away their transgressions: "And what is this bleating of the sheep in my ears; and the lowing of the oxen that I hear?"

Saul seems unperturbed. His response is straightforward:

> They brought those from the Amalekites, for the people spared the best of the sheep and the oxen to sacrifice to the Lord your God; but the rest we have utterly destroyed.

Note several key terms here: "They brought those ..." — not "we" but "they." And: "The people spared the best..." — not "I spared ..."

Saul is separating himself from the transgression: the people did it, not he. Furthermore, adds Saul, their intentions were good. They did not do this out of selfish motives, for they do not intend to keep the spoils for themselves. They will serve as a "sacrifice to the Lord ..." Besides, "and the rest we did destroy."

Note also the use of "your God," not "our God" or just simply "God." Is Saul distancing himself from Samuel's God who asked him not to be merciful? Is Saul — consciously or not — showing a strain of rebellion as he begins to realize the gravity of his sin? Is his rationalization beginning to evaporate, only to be replaced by a subtle sense of resentment at having been asked to do what is for him so difficult: to refrain from exercising his quality of mercy?

As for this quality of mercy, another question emerges: is it possible that here we have an illustration of a mercy that is misguided? Saul is, after all, a descendant of Rachel, the embodiment of mercy. Recall that it was Rachel who performed a heroic act of compassion on behalf of her sister Leah who — through Laban's trickery — had become the substitute bride of Jacob in place of Rachel (Genesis 29:22-25). Jacob, who knew that Laban was fully capable of precisely such trickery, of substituting one sister for the other, had given Rachel a secret code — a kind of password — that would guarantee that his bride was truly Rachel. At the wedding, Rachel was fearful that her sister would be discovered and humiliated, and so, in a supreme act of selflessness, she provided Leah with the secret code (*Talmud Megillah* 13b; *Bava Batra* 123a). Rachel is thus the embodiment of mercy and pity. And in fact, when the prophet Jeremiah much later laments the exile of the Jewish people from their land, the Biblical figure who "weeps for her children" is none other than Rachel (Jeremiah 31:14).

Mercy and compassion are thus an integral part of the genes of Saul. Perhaps it is this very strain of mercy within Saul that lies behind Samuel's urgent "have no pity on him."

Mercy, after all, needs a framework; it is not without limits, and cannot be applied universally and haphazardly. It may be true that it "droppeth as the gentle rain from heaven," but it requires boundaries. The doctor who takes pity on his patient and refuses to cut his skin to remove a tumor is ultimately not being merciful. Similarly, it is possible that when Saul spares Agag, he is wrongfully applying the quality of mercy. God wants Agag, the representation of evil, to be eliminated. God is the Author of mercy. He is the "God who is merciful and compassionate, long-suffering, filled with lovingkindness and goodness..." (Exodus 34:6). As the embodiment and the fountainhead of all mercy, He can demand of His creatures, when necessary, an occasional suspension of this quality — as He does in the commandment to put to death those who incite the people to idolatry: "Your eye shall not pity him, and you shall have no mercy" (Deuteronomy 13: 9). There, God uses the very same words that Samuel uses here: *lo tachmol*. The human interpretation of mercy cannot be the touchstone by which the Divine command is or is not implemented. Mercy requires a mooring in something beyond the subjective self. (See *Yoma* 22b for further discussion of Saul's subjective mercy.)

This, incidentally, is not the first bitter confrontation between Samuel and Saul. In chapter 13, Saul had violated an earlier command. Samuel had informed Saul that he must wait seven days before the battle with the Philistines, and that Samuel would bring an offering to God when he returns after the seven days. Saul waits until the seventh day, but not the full seven days, and, fearful and impatient, brings the offering himself before Samuel arrives.

When Samuel finally arrives and discovers that Saul has not waited for him, he asks Saul a simple, two-worded question: *Meh asita* — "What have you done?"

This is not a question that solicits information. Samuel knows full well what Saul has done. This question is an accusation. It is reminiscent of the question that Moses, in Exodus 32:21, asks his brother Aaron after the incident of the Golden Calf, using almost the identical words: *Meh asa lecha ha-am ha-zeh* — "What has this people done to you?" — although Moses, unlike Samuel, directs part of the accusation at "the people," not at Aaron alone.

What have you done? Do you comprehend fully the implications of your actions?

Saul attempts to explain: He had waited, but it did not seem that Samuel would arrive in time; furthermore, his troops were deserting him en masse, the heavily armed Philistines were in the hills above them and the Israelite camp was down in the valley; he was fearful of an imminent attack, and he felt that now was the time to approach God through this offering (Samuel 13:11-12).

Samuel is unmoved. He is not a man of many words. He replies with one terrible word: *Niskalta* — "You have acted foolishly." He goes on to warn Saul that because of Saul's violation of the prophet's command, he will lose his kingship, and that God will find "a man after his own heart" to be king of Israel (ibid. 13:14). And later, when Saul again transgresses by violating the commandment not to spare anyone in the camp of Amalek, the final and climactic note is struck in the tragedy of Saul's kingship. (See commentary of R. David Qimhi on I Samuel 15:28, and of Ralbag on 15:23, in which both of Saul's violations are discussed.)

Why does Saul — whom the text describes as "head and shoulders higher above all the people" (I Samuel 9:2) seem to dissemble to Samuel? And how is it that this great king of Israel seems to blame it all on the people who, he claims, prevailed over him?

The answer, as we have seen, is that Saul is not trying to deceive anyone. He is convinced that he has done the right thing.

In this respect, Saul — the towering spiritual giant who had been granted divine inspiration, whom the Bible calls the *bechir Yisrael* — "the chosen one of Israel" (II Samuel 21:6); who, like

Moses himself, is characterized by the Bible as being *tov* — "good" (Exodus 2:2; I Samuel 9:2); who the Talmud describes as the pre-eminent Torah scholar of his time (*Gittin* 59a); who possesses unlimited possibilities for sanctifying the Name of the God of Israel — is quintessentially human. And, like a human, his ability to rationalize, to justify his actions even when they are wrong, is also unlimited.

It is perfectly normal to claim innocence before our Maker. We did no wrong, we claim. We did our best. When God reminds us that we closed our eyes to that poor man; that we slandered an innocent person; that we bent the truth in order to make a greater profit — *Oh, that? That was nothing: that man whom I slandered had it coming to him. That person I cheated was himself a cheat and deserved it. I admit that I did wrong, but it only happened a few times, and I know it was not right, but there were special circumstances that forced me to do it. I didn't make a habit of it. True, I violated most of the rest of the commandments, and I rarely even bothered to pray, and when I did pray I mouthed words without thinking what I was saying — but I was very busy providing for my family. That, too, is a mitzvah, is it not?*

Normal rationalizations, yes. But each rationalization is confronted by Samuel's piercing question: "What is this bleating of the sheep in my ears?" No amount of excuses and rationalizations can blot out the sounds of the bleating sheep. The evidence of the sin does not evaporate; it remains hanging in the air.

But a human being finds ways to explain misdeeds, to rationalize, to justify one's own failings and turn them into righteous deeds. As for the bleating of the sheep: first we do not hear it, then we ignore it, then we explain it away, and then we justify it and transform it into a positive good.

Saul, first king of Israel, the chosen one of God, he who is head and shoulders above all of Israel, meets his final downfall because of his inability to see his error. Nor can he answer that other piercing question of Samuel: "What have you done?"

This is an object lesson to all lesser people: if self-justification and blindness to the implications of one's deeds can destroy a man as great as Saul, how much more so should ordinary people be vigilant.

This is why Judaism places such great value on the penitent. For an essential ingredient of true *teshuvah* — repentance — the ability to admit clearly and unequivocally that one has gone astray. Those who are able to admit fully that their actions have not met the guidelines of God; who are able to turn their backs on their past and to move forward in a direction that is infused by what God wants and not by what they themselves want — such people are overcoming their basic human instincts. Instead of justifying themselves, they are turning themselves around and pointing to a different future. And this is why the Sages refer to such people in glowing terms, going so far as to state that even the most righteous of men cannot be compared to a genuine penitent (see *Berachot* 34b).

There are two kinds of people: those who are able to hear the bleating of the sheep, and those who do not hear.

It would take us far afield to discuss the following in depth, but it must be addressed: Why should Saul be so severely punished — to have his kingship taken from him — for not waiting for the prophet Samuel? After all, what was the great transgression that he committed? He merely offered up an *olah* sacrifice to God — an offering from which he had no personal gain since it is entirely consumed on the altar — in violation of the command that only Samuel should offer that sacrifice. But observe the supreme pressure under which Saul was operating that day. As he himself explains, his troops were deserting, the overwhelming enemy was on a nearby hill, and despite this he had waited almost the full seven days for the prophet.

But all this is as nothing before Samuel. You violated the divine edict; therefore you will be replaced by another king. (Samuel uses the unusual term *niskalta* — "foolish" — chastising Saul, and not something seemingly more appropriate such as "evil" or "rebellious" or "unfaithful". Perhaps this is because the prophet knows that Saul is not evil, or rebellious, or unfaithful to God: rather, he has foolishly rationalized why he should not follow the Divine instruction, as suggested in *Yoma* 22b.)

There was an earlier moment in Jewish history when a serious transgression took place for similar reasons. In Exodus 32:1, "the people saw that Moses delayed coming down from the mountain ...." They insist that Aaron make for them a god who will lead them, "because we do not know what has become of this man Moses." A golden calf is made, and the Israelites "eat and drink and disport themselves" (ibid. 32:6).

What the Israelites did in the desert and what Saul did are both violations. But compare the two sins. The Israelites in the desert made for themselves an idol; but Saul's transgression was that he offered up a premature sacrifice — not to an idol but to the One God! Despite this, and despite the anger of his brother Moses, Aaron is not stripped of his leadership role. (There is indirect evidence that were it not for the intercession of Moses, God would have destroyed Aaron: in his farewell address to Israel, Moses says, referring to the Calf, that "God was very angry with Aaron to have destroyed him, but I prayed for Aaron ..." (Deuteronomy 9:20).

In any case, Aaron retains his role, but Saul is stripped of his leadership — for a seemingly much lesser and a much more understandable offense.

Is it because Aaron was not personally responsible for the making of the Calf, and in fact made an effort to delay its building — while Saul's action was his alone?

Is it because Aaron was not the king of the Israelites, and that a king of Israel like Saul is judged by a more severe standard than is a *kohen*?

Is it because God was reluctant in the first place to have a monarchy over Israel (I Samuel 8:7), and that in any case monarchy had been promised to the lineage of Judah — i.e. David — and not the lineage of Benjamin — i.e. Saul — as stated in Genesis 49:10: "The rod [of kingship] shall not depart from Judah?" (See also Nachmanides at Genesis 49:10, s.v. *Lo tasur shevet miYehudah).*

Is it because Saul does not deport himself as befits a king, allowing commoners to degrade his office (*Yoma* 22b) so that Samuel admonishes him in (I Samuel 15:17): "Though you are small in your own eyes, you are the head of the tribes of Israel, and the Lord anointed you king over Israel"?

Is it because he ultimately admits that "I feared the people and obeyed their voice"? (ibid. 15:24)

Is it because he does not immediately accept responsibility for his actions, and instead tries to explain that the troops were deserting, Samuel did not appear, the enemy was massing? This characteristic emerges once again in the fatal encounter with Samuel after the Amalek battle. There, again, Saul also does not accept personal responsibility, blaming it all on the people. But we must note that neither does Aaron accept responsibility for the Calf (Exodus 32:22-24).

But lest it appear that God plays favorites with Aaron or his brother Moses, note another incident in which the Divine command is not faithfully followed. In Numbers 20:8, after the Israelites complain about the lack of water, God says to Moses, "Take the rod ... speak to the rock before their eyes, and it shall give forth water ...." But Moses does not speak to the rock. Instead, he strikes it twice with the rod in his hand until the water emerges. Here, God's retribution is swift. Moses and Aaron are not asked why they did what they did; there is no discussion which might give them a chance to explain. In the very next verse, God says to Moses and Aaron: "Because you did not believe in Me to sanctify Me in the eyes of the Children of Israel, therefore you shall not bring them into the land which I have given them" (ibid. 20:12). Involved here, of course, is more than the breaking of a command. What is involved is the missed opportunity to sanctify publicly the Name of God. Whatever the considerations, however, we find that Saul is not the only leader who is severely punished for not following the Divine command.

There is, of course, the case of King David. For his behavior concerning the husband of BatSheba he does not lose his kingdom. In *Midrash Tehillim* at Psalm 27, the ministering angels ask God why He removed the kingship from Saul and not from David. God replies that in times of crisis, David regularly asked for Divine guidance, while Saul did not. Contrast, incidentally, Saul's behavior with that of King David when the prophet Nathan accuses him of transgressing. Without hesitation, David admits his sin (II Samuel 12:7, 13 and also R. Y. Albo, *Sefer HaIkarim,* 4:26, for further analysis of this issue.)

(For a more detailed discussion of the exact nature of King David's transgression, see the end of chapter 5, "The Beginning of Regret: Is My Sin Too Great to Bear?")

18

What profit is there in my blood,
when I go down to the grave?

Psalms 30:10

GOD IN NEED OF MAN: *WHAT PROFIT IN MY DEATH?*

This searing plea to God must be read in its full context. In this psalm, David is singing a song of thanksgiving to God Who has saved him from near death and extinction. He recalls how he cried out to God and how God rescued him from the grave and kept him in life (vv. 3-4). In verse 10, David recounts the heart-rending words that he used in his prayer to God to keep him alive. It is an exquisite, perfectly formed prayer:

> *Mah betza' bedami* — What profit is there in my blood,
> *Berideti el shachat* — when I go down to the grave;
> *Hayodecha 'afar* — can dust acknowledge You,
> *Hayagid amitecha* — can it relate Your truth?

In examining this question and this prayer, certain crucial truths emerge about the relationship between man and God.

On one level, David is pleading for his own life. But on another, he is pleading for the life of all of Israel. (A case can also be made that at bottom this is a plea to God to reverse His original decree of death for all mankind — the result of the trangression of Adam and Eve — but that requires a separate discussion.)

What good will it do if I — or the Jewish people — die; what purpose will be served if we cease to exist? Who else will praise You, offer psalms of thanksgiving, and spread Your teachings to the entire world? Neither I nor the people Israel is perfect, says David, but You need us to sing the songs of Your greatness, to spread the love of You to all of Your creatures. Should we cease to exist, who will be left to demonstrate Your greatness and power and lovingkindness? What does it profit You to bring us down into the grave? Perhaps we deserve to die, but no one will gain from this — and You, O God and Master, will lose, for You will be diminished in Your own world.

Granted, all of creation can sing Your praises, but only Israel knows You well. And while the inanimate creation can praise You — and they do — of what value are such praises?

Hayodecha 'afar? Can dust thank You or praise You or acknowledge You or tell of Your truth? A clod of earth that has no choice but to be a clod of earth — of what value is its gratitude or its praise or its acknowledgment?

Granted, I am also from the dust, but You have endowed this piece of dust with a soul and with a mind that transforms me into a living human being. Alive, I possess many choices and endless possibilities. If I choose, I can even turn aside from You. Only a human being who is tempted to turn aside from You and does not — only his acknowledgment means something. And only such acknowledgment can bring Your reality into Your universe; only such praise can be a true witness to Your everlasting Presence.

But when life comes to an end, the soul's task as servant of God comes to an end as well; and although the soul returns to You and endures forever, it can no longer serve You or sing before You. If my soul is removed from me and I become again a clod of dust that praises You — that praise means very little.

This is an urgent plea for life. Note what David stresses when he wants to stress the importance of life. He comes down to essentials. The purpose of life is not simply to eat, or to have pleasure, or to exercise power over others. The purpose of life is to attune ourselves so that we can see the Presence of God at every moment of life, and, seeing Him, to acknowledge this Presence in a thousand different ways. When a human being sees all that God has prepared for him, and recognizes the beauty and care and order and sustenance of the physical universe around him; when he experiences God's Presence

> in the garden rose,
> in the soaring bird,
> in the leaf of a tree,
> in the blade of grass,
> in the power of the sun,
> in the exquisite form of a snowflake,
> in the life-giving rain,
> in the powerful oceans and raging rivers
> and vast, endless deserts,
> in the soaring vault of heaven above,
> and in its galaxies of stars and planets,
> in the depths of the sea below,
> in the mountains reaching toward the sky,
> in the life force within the tiny insect,
> in the birth of a child,
> in human love and goodness —

when one is able to sense these things, all else fades into insignificance. One is overwhelmed by His Presence, and one can only respond by recounting His glory, singing His praises, and submitting himself to God's will and sovereignty.

Who in all of God's vast creation is able to see all this and acknowledge God as the Author of it all? Only man. And among men, Israel as the chosen one of God is best positioned to witness His Presence in the universe. And if a man dies, or if Israel were to become extinct, God would somehow be diminished. As David says it in similar words in a later Psalm, (88:12): "Will your kindness be related in the grave....?

The word *betza*, translated as "profit," or "gain," contains a spiritual and moral connotation when used in relationship to God. But it is a decidedly indelicate term in its other uses in the Bible. Judah, for example, convinces his brothers not to kill Joseph because (using the identical formulation) *mah betza* — "what profit is there if we kill our brother....?" (Genesis 37:26) That is, we have nothing to gain by so doing, whereas if we sell him as a slave, we do have something to gain. Moses is commanded to choose as his associates "men of truth, who hate *betza* ...", who hate tainted gain (Exodus 18:21). Jeremiah decries those who would do anything for *betza* (Jeremiah 6:13).

King David's use of *betza* in connection with God — that God will not profit from our death — is on the surface extremely bold and irreverent — perhaps a sign of desperate pleading. What does it profit You if You put us to death? What do You have to gain from it?

Perhaps David is pointing out a profound truth here: that God without man has lost something critical in His universe. Would it really matter to God, would His power be lessened were we no longer to exist? To this, David answers with a resounding Yes!

On the face of it, the Creator is all-powerful and has no need of other forces in the universe. But in his use of the term *betza*, David is suggesting something quite startling: that God would in fact be diminished if we were to disappear. For David is reminding God that, for His own mysterious reasons, He has appointed man to be His representative and His caretaker in the world He created, and that there exists a partnership between man and God. In Genesis 1:28, man is told to "replenish the earth and subdue it"; and in Genesis 2:15, man is placed in the Garden of Eden "to till it and to protect it." That man needs God goes without saying. But now that God has appointed man to be the caretaker of His creation and to be, as it were, His earthly partner, it turns out that God, as it were, also needs man.

This concept is expanded upon later in the Torah. God makes a covenant — the *berit* — with Abraham and later with the people, Israel. In this *berit*, God promises to sustain Israel and the universe if Israel promises to sustain God's Presence in this universe. God will be our God and we will be His people. Specifically, if we subject ourselves to Him, if we become His ambassadors to introduce His teachings to the world, and if we perform His Divine will, He will sustain us and protect us.

If Israel and God are partners in creation, then by definition each needs the other. And if Israel were to cease to exist, God would not only lose His earthly caretaker; He would also lose the one vehicle on earth that can carry the message of God to all mankind. True, argues David, we may be unworthy partners, but partners we are nonetheless. No one else can fill our role. Therefore, what does it profit You, O God, if we disappear:

> *What profit is there in my blood,*
> *When I go down to the grave;*
> *Can dust acknowledge You,*
> *Can it relate Your truth?*

From King David, the Psalmist, we learn how to pray to our Creator, particularly when circumstances are difficult. While petitionary prayer is only one of several approaches to our Creator — there are also prayers of praise, of gratitude, of recognition of God's might and power — petitionary prayer is definitely a major component of prayer. One should never be shy in asking for what one needs. God wants to hear our prayers, and desires that we should connect with Him and develop a genuine relationship with Him. One must be respectful before God, obviously; but within one's shyness, one can also be bold and knock on His door again and again.

But note that David does not merely ask for life. He promises something in return: if he is granted life, he will be able to continue to acknowledge and sing to God. This is a vital paradigm of prayer. It is a reaching out to God and an attempt to establish a connection with Him. Each of us, like David, can pledge to sing to God in one's own special way: through meaningful charity, or the deeper observance of a mitzvah, or the adoption of a neglected mitzvah, or greater concentration in prayer, or an effort to understand the weaknesses and foibles of others, or the setting aside of special time for the study of God's Torah.

The institution of formal, structured prayer was established when the ancient Temple in Jerusalem was destroyed, and stands in lieu of the discontinued Temple offerings. Although God welcomes us even if we come empty-handed, we should approach Him by offering something in return.

God wants our prayer, whether formal or informal, whether structured or not. He desires it not for His sake but for our sake — for when we acknowledge Him, we become better partners in His creation. He wants to keep us in life, for He knows that only Israel can properly acknowledge Him. He would rather that His living creatures, and not clods of inanimate earth, reach out to Him.

What profit is there in my blood
When I go down to the grave?
Can dust acknowledge You,
can it relate Your truth?

19

By the rivers of Babylon, there we sat
and we also wept when we remembered Zion.
Upon the willows in her midst
had we hung up our harps.
For there our captors demanded of us
words of song,
and those that mocked us, joy:
"Sing for us from a song of Zion."

Eich nashir et shir haShem
How can we sing the Lord's song
on the soil of the stranger?
If I forget you, O Jerusalem,
may my right hand fail,
may my tongue cleave to my mouth
if ever I do not recall You,
if ever I do not place Jerusalem
at the pinnacle of my joy....

Psalms 137:4-6

THE MEANING OF MELODY: *HOW CAN WE SING THE LORD'S SONG ON THE SOIL OF THE STRANGER?*

You who are our enemies, you do not understand. To you, one land is the same as another. To you it makes little difference where one's abode is. It is all the same earth, the same grass, the same fields, the same water, the same sheep and cattle. So you demand that we sing for you "a song of Zion."

In response, we tell you that we cannot sing "the song of the Lord" — because for us the song of the Lord and the song of Zion are one and the same. The songs of Zion are not merely songs of a distant, exotic land, as you seem to think; they are the songs of the Lord, songs of holiness and joy. Such songs cannot find expression in any other land but the land of God. There will be no songs of Zion for you, our captors, for the songs of Zion are in fact the songs of the Lord.

In truth, you do not seek music and song from us. You seek entertainment, amusement, laughter, merriment. But our singing — our *shirah* — is not a entertainment. Rather, its purpose is to praise the Lord in thanksgiving.

Not only is music not an entertainment for us; it even transcends ordinary aesthetics. For us, music is the ladder upon which we climb upward towards God. It detaches us and separates us from the world of the merely physical, so that we can rise up towards the spiritual. Music opens us up and enables us to receive the spirit of holiness from above. That is why music and singing are integral elements of our prayers to God. The entire book of Psalms, which forms so much of our daily worship, is a book of songs to the Creator. Similarly, when we study our Torah as part of our worship, that, too, is done through chanting and melodic cadences. In fact, R. Akiva urges everyone to study the words of Torah by singing them, even outside the context of prayer: "Sing it every day, sing it every day." (*Sanhedrin* 99a-b) Even the angels sing before Him daily, says the Talmud (*Hagiga* 14a).

Song possesses a mysterious power to cut away the entangling underbrush that prevents us from reaching God. For example, the Hebrew word, *zemer*, is one of the words for "song". But it also means "to prune" and "to cut away". This is a hidden meaning of the term in Isaiah 25:5: *zemir aritzim* — "cut away the branches"

— cut away by using *zemer* — song — in order to be able to reach out to God. Through song and melody we become one with God. A major section of our morning prayer is called *pesukei dezimrah* — "passages of song" — because it consists of selections from the book of Psalms. But it also means "passages of cutting away": it disposes of anything that interferes with our contact with God. So crucial is music to reaching out to God that our Levites spent five years of training to learn how to produce their melodies that accompanied the Temple offerings to God.

Music is so powerful a force that even the prophets of Israel needed it to bring upon themselves the spirit of God. Thus, I Samuel 10:5 describes a veritable orchestra of prophets: "a band of prophets coming down from the high places with a lute and timbrel and a pipe and a lyre before them, and they shall prophesy...." That is because our prophets could only prophesy when they were in a state of *simcha* — "joy" (see *Shabbat* 30b). If someone who possessed the Divine Spirit became despondent, the Divine Spirit departed from him until the sadness dissipated. This is why our father Jacob temporarily lost that Spirit while he was in mourning over the disappearance of his son Joseph.

And when King Saul becomes melancholy, and the spirit of the Lord departs from him, his loyal servants suggest that he bring before him a certain *menagen* — "musician" (who turns out to be the future King David, sweet-singer of Israel). For the sound of music will restore to Saul the Divine Spirit that had been lifted from him (see I Samuel 16:14-22).

We find further, in II Kings 3:15, that Elisha the prophet says, "Bring me a musician — a *menagen* — and as the musician played — *kenagen hamenagen* — then the hand of the Lord came upon him."

This is why the Talmud states that "the *Ruach Hakodesh* —the Divine Spirit — rests on those who are engaged in the joy of a mitzvah" (*Shabbat* 3a). And the Jerusalem Talmud (see *Sukkah* 5:1) reports that the Divine Spirit was present during the intense joy of the *simchat beit hasho-evah* — the water-libation ceremony — during the festival of Sukkot.

It is clear, then, that music possesses an extraordinary power for us. Even nature has its own music and celebrates the Creator, as it states in Job 38:7: "the morning stars sang together ...." The Talmud echoes this in *Rosh Hashanah* 8a, in which it speaks of "the song of the ears of grain," while Jerusalem Talmud in *Chagiga* 2:1 refers to "trees bursting into song."

You, our captors, ask us to sing for you — but for you, music and song are the instruments of debased orgies and, at best, drunken revelries, which our sacred books describe in disgust (see *Sotah* 48b, citing Isaiah ch. 5).

But for us, *shirah* reflects the harmony and union of the two great opposing forces in the universe: heaven and earth, the spiritual and the physical. Genuine *shirah* occurs when these opposites unite as one.

The sound of our *shofar*, for example, is for us a sublime means of connecting ourselves with the Creator. For you, it is only a mundane noise that emanates when one blows into the horn of an animal. But when a Jew hears the sound of the *shofar*, his soul also hears the sound of Sinai — *kol hashofar* (see Exodus 19:16). That sound represents the harmony of the universe, the sound of worlds uniting as one, of Abraham and Isaac reaching out for God together on Mount Moriah, of the Messiah ushering in a new world of oneness and peace.

This is why — when you, our captors, ask us to sing for you — our response is *Eich nashir* — "How can we sing ...." That word, *Eich,* does not only mean "how". That word is a cry of pain and of longing, part of that awe-filled word of mourning and lament, *Eichah*. We cannot sing when we are in a state of mourning; we can only lament.

You mock us by asking us to sing, but you mock us for the wrong reasons. It is not only that we are exiles, and exiles do not sing joyous songs. We cannot sing because our souls are not at peace anywhere in the world but in that special land and in that special place. For once a Jew has experienced the glory of the Holy Temple, once he has witnessed the majesty of the offerings, and the glory of the Kohanim and Levites, and seen the splendor of Jerusalem on its festive days, there can be no singing and no joy in any other place. Jerusalem is "the perfection of beauty, the joy of the whole earth," says Lamentations 2:15. He who has never seen the Temple in its full manifestation has never seen a glorious structure in his life, say our Sages (*Sukkah* 51b); and so lovely was the city that of the ten portions of beauty that descended from heaven onto the earth, nine portions were given to Jerusalem (*Kiddushin* 49b).

But it is not only its physical beauty that has been destroyed. It is the lifeline to our Creator that has been disrupted. Jerusalem was the starting point that enabled us to touch God's Presence. The Holy Temple was the medium through which we were able to reach up to our God and to sense a closeness and intimacy with Him. For only of Jerusalem do the Sages declare that this is Jacob's "gateway to heaven" (Genesis 28:17) that is always open to those who genuinely seek God.

You, our captors, will never understand that the soul of the Jew is attached to the Holy Land by a spiritual umbilical cord that extends back to the Patriarchs and to God's repeated promise to give us the Land as an inheritance. Upon its every grain of sand rests the imprint of the Creator. "The eyes of the Lord are upon [the Land] from the beginning of the year until the end of the year," says our Torah in Deuteronomy 11:12. For us, the Land is unlike any other place. It is not simply our homeland. That would make our absence tragic enough. It is also the homeland, so to speak, of our Creator, the dwelling place of the *Shechinah*, the Presence of God Himself. That is why the Land is the only place where the soul of the Jew is tranquil and at peace.

Now all that is gone. We are not only distant from our Holy City; we are distant from our Holy God. All that remains now for us are the mediums of Torah, mitzvot, and prayer, which we cherish and which we invest with all of our spiritual energies. All else have you taken away from us. And now you ask us to sing and to be joyous? This is among your great, mocking cruelties.

For only when one is tranquil and at peace can one sing. One cannot sing when one is exposed and vulnerable and unprotected — all of which is implicit in the Hebrew word for exile, *Galut*, from the word *galui*, "exposed". On foreign soil one weeps; one does not sing. In exile, the Jewish soul begins to shrivel, and the wellsprings of song and joy dry up. That is why our harps are hanging on the willows by the rivers of Babylon. We have no more need for harps. Not only do we have no desire to make music when we are in exile; we lack even the ability to make music.

Certainly we know how to sing and how to be joyous. Listen to our singing at our great moments of triumph, whenever the hand of the Lord has been made visible for us. At the miracle of the Sea of Reeds, Moses and the Children of Israel explode into song. Or listen to the glorious song of Deborah in Judges ch. 5, at her triumphant victory over the mighty Sisera, or to the singing of the women in I Samuel 18:6-7 as they welcome the triumphant return of David and Saul with "singing and dancing ... with timbrels and joyous song and with lutes." Our Bible describes numerous kinds of musical instruments: pipes and trumpets and lyres and cymbals and lutes and bells and drums and harps. The Mishnah (*Bikkurim* 2:4) vividly describes the joyous processional of First Fruits that are brought up to Jerusalem, an event in which *simcha* and *shirah* play pivotal roles. It is no wonder that we explode into joyous song at our festivals and joyous moments. So pervasive is song and music in our lives that the Talmud denigrates him "who reads [the Torah] without melody and who studies [Mishnah] without song" (*Megillah* 32a).

We know how to sing, but we also know when and where and why to sing. *Shirah* is the Hebrew word for such songs — songs of joy and praise and triumph and thanksgiving to our Creator. That which cannot be articulated in ordinary words can often be expressed in music and song, either verbal or instrumental. Music is a reflection of the soul, an expression of inner longings, hopes, joys, or profound sadness.

We know how to sing. In the Temple offering service, the offerings were accompanied by joyous singing. And the Levites sang a special song for each day of the week, a song that is still recited in the daily prayers of the Jew.

Joy — *simcha* — and song permeate our sacred books. In our Bible, the root word for song, *shir*, appears over one hundred-fifty times, and various forms of the root word for joy/*simcha* (*sin*, *mem*, *ches*) are found over two hundred-fifty times. We know how to engage ourselves in simcha. Our Torah often commands us to "be joyous in your festivals, and you shall be *ach sameach* — "extremely joyous". The book of Psalms, in 100:2, declares, "Serve the Lord *besimcha* — in joy, — come before Him *birenana* — in glad song." And in an astonishing reproof, Deuteronomy 28:47 informs us that one of our greatest sins is that although we served the Lord, we "did not serve the Lord with joy ...."

Some of our most profound teachings are written as songs. In the last words of Moses to Israel — in which he imparts his great vision to the people Israel, celebrating our past and envisioning our future, encouraging us to remain forever loyal to the God of Israel — even the written text in the Torah is written in the physical form of a poem. The Torah itself introduces this chapter by referring to it as a *Shirah* (Deuteronomy 31:30). In fact, some traditions suggest that the entire Torah is in itself a *Shirah*, for the Torah itself is a song of praise to God (*Sanhedrin* 21a). As King David writes in Psalms 119:54, "Your statutes, O God, have been my songs during my pilgrimages."

Shirah in the Bible connotes harmony, a blend of different sounds flowing together in one melodic whole. Our Kabbalists write that every element of the universe combines with every other element in one chorus of song which together create an echo of the unseen world. Each element of creation — even the tiny blade of grass — sings its own song, and each geographical area its own divine melody. Thus, when Genesis 43:11 recounts Jacob's instructions to his sons to bring a gift to the Viceroy of Egypt, the gift they are to bring is one of song. Although *k'chu mi-zimrat ha-aretz bik-*

leichem is normally translated as "take of the Land's glory in your containers," the kabbalists read *mi-zimrat* more subtly, perceiving in it the root word for "song", *zemer*: "take from the melody of the Land." (Rashi here anticipates this reading when, based on Onkelos — who consistently translates *shirah* as *tushbechaya* — "praise" — he translates Jacob's words as: "take that of which everyone sings (*mezamrim*) its praises....")

Although each aspect of creation sings its own song, they sing continuously together in profound praise of their Master and Creator. Thus all of nature is a manifestation of Heavenly melody, for in it all the disparate elements of the universe come together in exquisite precision, in a symphony of harmony and cooperation. The music of God's world is designed to be the very opposite of discord and cacophony. (See commentary of Beit HaLevi on Exodus 15:1 — the Song of the Sea — concerning the connection between this Song and the ultimate harmony of the universe.)

But while the natural universe is whole and harmonious, there is discord in the human universe, and from time to time there is cacophony in our relationship with our own Master. There is no greater discord than hatred and war and suffering and exile. At such times, the melody of harmony is transformed into laments that give expression to discord.

As a people, we are not strangers to sad songs and laments. But we do not call these *Shirah*. We call these *nehi* and *kinah*. The *Shirah* of joy reflects the rhythm and cadence of vibrant life. But the *nehi* and *kinah* of lament and dirge bear the jagged edge and dissonance of tragedy. An entire sacred book of ours, the book of *Eichah*, Lamentations, is devoted to lamenting the loss of our holy places. Jeremiah speaks of such sad songs. He refers to the *mekonenot*, professional mourning women whose wailing engenders deep sadness among the listeners (Jeremiah 9:15). We Jews can readily chant before you these laments for Zion, but we cannot sing the songs of Zion.

But, you say, other peoples have been exiled, and they have soon enough become reconciled to their fate, blotted out the memories of their homeland, and made new permanent homes in the lands of their exile. Why are you such a stubborn people, refusing to forget?

This is because we are unlike any other people. To be stubborn and stiff-necked can be a positive trait. We are stubborn, so that wherever we wander in our exile, our prayers are directed towards Jerusalem. We are stiff-necked, so that we refer to Jerusalem in all of our prayers, and turn our faces in her direction whenever we pray. We are in perpetual mourning for Jerusalem, even when we live in strange lands. In our dwelling places, we leave a bare, unplastered space on the inside wall facing the entrance. There are among us many who — although they are fortunate enough to live in the as yet unredeemed Jerusalem — do not play instrumental music even at weddings. Only the sound of drums accompanying a singer is heard, so that in the very midst of our joy, the fallen glory of the Jerusalem that once was remains at the pinnacle of our thoughts. We interrupt the joyous moments of our weddings by shattering a glass, to remind ourselves that as long as Jerusalem and our Temple are still not rebuilt, our happiness is shattered and incomplete. When we approach the last remaining vestige of our ancient Temple — the Western Wall — we rend our garments, like people in mourning. And we have special days of fasting and remembrance to mark the various stages of our destruction — climaxed by the full-day fast of the Ninth of Av, in which we chant the entire book of Lamentations as well as numerous dirges and *kinnot*. "If I forget you, O Jerusalem, may my tongue cleave to my mouth" (Psalms 137:5) — this is not merely a phrase; for us it is a daily reality. We are, as you note, very stubborn, very stiff-necked.

We will some day engage in true *Shirah*; some day we will have genuine *simcha*. We anxiously await the time of our redemption. Then all the world will understand why the great song of Moses at the Sea is introduced by the future tense: *Az yashir Moshe uv'nei*

Yisroel — "Then Moses and the Children of Israel will sing ...."
The use of the future tense to describe an event that has already
transpired is unusual. One would expect to hear the past tense:
"sang." What it means is that on that special day in the future our
enemies will understand, and then they will also realize why we
refused to sing the songs of Zion until that time.

On that day, we will reclaim our harps from the willows, our
hearts will overflow with the genuine joy of return, and our mouths
will be filled with words of song.

But until that time, *Eich nashir* — "How can we sing?..."

20

Why are all those tranquil
who deal treacherously ...?

Jeremiah 12:1

... Justice comes forth perverted.

Habakkuk 1:4

ULTIMATE QUESTIONS TO THE ULTIMATE ONE: *WHY DO THE WICKED PROSPER?*

The question is as old as mankind. God is a God of justice. There is in His universe a system of reward and punishment. Why, then, do so many of the wicked seem to prosper, and so many of the righteous seem to suffer? Jeremiah puts it in direct terms:

Righteous are You, O Lord, therefore I could plead with You; yet must I speak of justice with You. Why does the way of the wicked prosper, why are all those tranquil who deal treacherously? You have planted them, they have taken root, they grow, they also bring forth fruit ... (Jeremiah 12:1).

Habakkuk begins his prophecy with a plangent cry (1:4):

Justice (mishpat) *does not come forth victorious, for the wicked encompass the righteous, therefore justice comes forth perverted.*
And in verse 13, he asks:

Lamah — *Why do You gaze upon those that deal treacherously, and are silent when the wicked swallows up him who is more righteous than he?"?*

The question of how to reconcile a just God with a world that seems so unjust, and how to reconcile a system of reward and punishment with a reality that at least on the surface seems to flout this system, has always agitated mankind. Abraham asks a similar question based on God's justice: if there are some righteous people in Sodom, would God, who is the source of all justice, destroy the righteous with the wicked? (Genesis 18:25). Moses specifically asks if God would actually destroy an entire community simply because one man had sinned (Numbers 16:22). And earlier, in Exodus 33:13, Moses asks God, "Show me Your ways," which the Gemara expands:

Moses said, Master of the universe, why are there righteous who have good lives, and other righteous who do not have good lives; and wicked who have good lives, and other wicked who do not have good lives? Replied He: the righteous whose lives are good are the righteous who are children of the righteous; the righteous whose lives are not good are the righteous who are children of the wicked. The wicked whose lives are good are the the wicked who are children of the righteous; the wicked whose lives are not good are the wicked who are children of the wicked .... Others say, the righteous whose lives are good — these are completely righteous; the righteous whose lives are not good — these are not completely righteous; the wicked whose lives are good — these are not completely wicked; the wicked whose lives are not good — these are the completely wicked (Berachot 7a).

R. Jannai in Avot 4:14 says quite simply:

It is not in our power (lit: "it is not in our hands") to understand the tranquility of the wicked and the suffering of the righteous.

Rashi on this Avot text adds, citing the above passage in Jeremiah, "It is not known why the way of the wicked prospers." Adds Rashi:

"It is not in our power to understand…for so would it seem in terms of justice (din), that the wicked should not have peace in this world, and the righteous should not suffer — but the matter is not given over to our hands, but is in the hands of the Holy One Blessed Be He ...."

Rashi goes on to suggest that full justice will be meted out in the World-to-Come, where the accounts of the wicked and the righteous will be properly balanced. In this, Rashi is echoing Avot 2:16: "The reward for the righteous is in the World-to-Come."

Elsewhere, our Sages grapple with this issue and resolve it in a similar fashion. They suggest that the righteous are punished in this world for the slightest transgressions, while the wicked are rewarded in this world for the slightest mitzvot, and that, conversely, the wicked are punished in the World-to-Come for their transgressions, while the righteous are rewarded in the world-to-come for their mitzvot (*Taanit* 11a). Both reward and punishment are of a much sharper intensity in the World-to-Come, and therefore the reward of the righteous is withheld until then, as is the punishment of the wicked.

In a similar vein, the Talmud (*Kiddushin* 39b) states that *s'char mitzvah behai alma leka* — "there is no reward in this world for a mitzvah." In other words, this mundane world is too small to contain the vast and limitless reward that is engendered by the performance of a mitzvah and by the living of a Godly life.

Furthermore, if it were clear that all the wicked are punished and all the righteous prosper, then man's freedom of choice would not be challenged. He who does God's will would simply be a panderer, since he knows in advance that he will be rewarded. By contrast, he who serves God without assurance of reward, even with the possibility of suffering despite his good works, is far more precious in the eyes of God than he who refrains from evil for fear of punishment, and does good in anticipation of a rich reward.

There is, in brief, justice in God's world, but it is hidden from view, just as the World-to-Come is hidden from view.

Something even more significant is hidden from view, and that is, of course, God Himself. By His very nature, He is unseen and intangible. Psalm 91:1, for example — which is often translated as "He that dwells in the secret place shall abide under the shadow of the Almighty" — can also be rendered as *Yoshev b'seter, Elyon* — "He [God] dwells in secret, the Most High"; *b'tzel, sh-dai yitlonan* — in a shadow does the Almighty abide." Concealment is an integral component of God's essence, which is one way to read Deuteronomy 29:28: *Hanistarot la-Shem ...* — "That which is hidden is God's ..." Proverbs 25:2 underscores this concept: "It is the glory of God to conceal (*haster*) a thing."

But not only is God invisible by His very nature. The Torah states that God will some day "hide My face from them ..." (Deuteronomy 31:17-18; 32:20; Ezekiel 39:23). This is the concept of *hester panim,* the concealment of God's Presence. The world will appear, says God, as if it has no God, as if I were absent. My mastery of the world will not be readily apparent. It will seem as if the forces of darkness, irrationality, and lunacy are in control of My universe.

This is perhaps the most terrifying of all the frightening admonitions in the Torah, as Rashi suggests in his explanation to Isaiah 8:17. For it can also be read to mean the following: I will turn aside from you and will allow the ship of the world to sail as if without a captain. I will permit the elements of evil, normally under My control, free rein. And when you seek Me, I will not readily be found, for My Presence will be hidden from you.

This leads to the fearful refrain of the Psalmist in 89:47: "How long, O God, will You hide Yourself forever?" and his outcry in Psalm 30:5: "You hid Your face, and I was confused" — how understandable these are! (See also Psalms 13:2; 27:9; 44:25; 69:18; 88:15; 102:3; 104:29; 119:10; 143:7.)

However, within this concept of *hester panim*/God's hidden face, as it were, there is some hidden solace, and that is that God is not in fact absent, but only hiding. Hiding is a temporary phenomenon, not an eternal one. Note that the Torah uses a doubling of the verb for "hidden" — *haster astir* (Deuteronomy 31:18) — usually translated as "I will surely hide," but that literally means "hide will I hide" — when one verb would have sufficed. It is doubled, writes R. Zadok HaKohen (*Pri Tzadik*, IV, s.v. *Purim*) to convey the idea that God will hide the fact that He is merely hiding, so that it will seem that He has in fact abandoned His world. But if we bear in mind that He hides but sees, and hides but cares, and hides but protects — that His concealment is not only temporary, but only apparent, and that He is actually present — then our faith is restored. Perhaps this is what is alluded to by Isaiah 54:8:

> With a slight wrath have I concealed My face (histarti panai) from you for a moment, but with eternal kindness will I show you mercy, says your Redeemer, the Lord.

God's concealment is not eternal; what is eternal are His kindness and mercy. But even a temporary dimming of His guiding Presence is terrifying enough — especially since a thousand years in God's eyes is "like a yesterday" (Psalms 90:4).

The entire book of Job struggles with the issue of God's justice, with each of Job's three friends attempting to comfort him with a solution — none of which satisfies him. At the beginning of the book, after Job suffers unspeakable misery and tragedy, his wife says to him, "Are you still holding fast to your integrity? Renounce God, and die." To which Job replies with a question: "Should we

Why Do the Wicked Prosper? □ 183

accept the good from God, and not the evil?" (2:9-10). In the book's awesome, climactic section, God speaks from the whirlwind and declares — through a series of penetrating and taunting questions — that His ways are too profound for the mortal, finite mind of man to comprehend:

> *Where were you when I laid the foundations of the earth ...?*
> *Who fixed her measurements ...?*
> *On what are her foundations placed at rest ...?*
> *Who closed up the doors of the sea ...?*
> *Did you ever command the morning ... or wander through the bottoms of the sea ...?*
> *Tell it if you know it all ...(Chap. 38 ff.).*

Viewed against the background of these closing chapters of Job, it becomes evident that questions about the Creator's system of justice are beyond our ken, and that R. Jannai in Avot says all that can be said on the subject: it is not in our power to understand. As God says to Moses when he asks to unlock the mystery: "You shall see My back, but My face will not be seen" (Exodus 33:20.) Here God's concealment is not a form of retribution to rebellious man; here it is simply a given fact in our relationship to the Creator. Man is incapable of understanding and comprehending the full nature and being of the Creator. We occasionally think He is absent when in fact He is standing next to us, unseen and unknown.

This is expressed in Psalms 77:20: "In the sea is Your way and Your path, in the many waters; but Your footsteps are not known." Read literally, this psalm refers to the miracle of the parting of the waters of the Red Sea: after the miracle and the destruction of the Egyptian pursuers, the waters returned to their original state, and no one could have known that God had manifested Himself upon these very waters. But in a broader sense, this psalm can also refer to God's works within His universe. He works quietly, invisibly, His "steps are not known." No one can be certain that God has been present all along, for He moves in silent and unknowable ways. For example, in the verse, *zeh sh'mi* — "this is My name — (i.e., My essence) *l'olam*

— forever (Exodus 3:15), the word *l'olam* can be translated differently — from the root *alm* — "concealed" — as in Leviticus 4:13, *v'neelam davar* — "the thing was hidden" and almost thirty other such uses in the Bible. Thus the verse can be read as "this is my name: concealment." (See Rashi ad loc, and *Kiddushin* 71a; cf. also *Midrash Tehillim* 9:1, commenting on Kohelet 3:11, *ha-olam*.) Similarly, the verse *ki l'olam chasdo* — "for his kindness is forever" (Psalms 136) can be read: "for his kindness is concealed."

Concealment of the full picture is the theme of this famous parable attributed to the Chafetz Chaim:

> *A man enters the synagogue in the midst of the Torah reading. The synagogue is filled with venerable and pious old men, but the one presently being honored by a call to the Torah is a very young man. The visitor confronts the Gabbai about this injustice. The Gabbai replies: "Obviously you do not know what transpired before you came in — when we gave great honor to the venerable men who are here. You have seen only part of the picture. Instead of criticizing, it would be better if you were a bit more patient."*

When we consider the impenetrable walls that are encountered when we set out to comprehend the mysteries of God, we begin to realize that perhaps God wants it this way. Quite possibly, He deliberately created us with limited tools of perception so that we should remain ignorant and uncomprehending; in all likelihood, He does not expect, nor desire, to be understood by us. As Proverbs puts it:

> *It is conceivable that we might never be able to reconcile our insistence that God is the Creator Who cares about His creatures and is concerned for their lives, with the ultimate agonizing question: how can He (apparently) look on silently as suffering takes place? "It is the glory of God to*

conceal a thing ..." (25:2). Perhaps He does not want us climbing up any walls or entering dark and mysterious caves from which there may be no way down or out. The Ineffable One wishes to remain ineffable.

Thus we are brought up short by the realization of this truth: only a god who is finite and mortal could be thoroughly comprehended by a finite and mortal mind; only an infinite and immortal mind can fathom the infinite and immortal God. We are faced with the incontrovertible fact that our minds are mortal and our God is immortal, hence He and His ways remain incomprehensible to us. Perhaps He would rather that we not expend our limited energies on theodicy, on mysteries beyond our ken, and on secrets beyond our mortal comprehension, but rather on living the life of holiness and service that He has outlined for us. Let the philosophical and theological problems rest in peace; they are best not disturbed until God Himself chooses, in the fullness of time, to unravel the mysteries for us. Perhaps in order to underscore this, the Talmud (*Hagigah* 14b) relates the cryptic incident of four great Sages — Ben Azai, Ben Zoma, Aher (Elisha b. Avuya), and R. Akiva — who entered the heavenly *pardes* (lit., "orchard") apparently to learn the mysteries of God, and especially why the righteous suffer). Of the four, only R. Akiva emerged whole and unscathed. The others were permanently damaged from "looking at God's face." *Ki lo yirani ha-adam vachai* — "for no man can gaze at me and live." (See end of Chapter 12 above).

One wonders if this is what King David has in mind when he says in Psalm 131:1-2:

I have not exercised myself in great matters or in things too wondrous for me (nifla-ot mimeni). Surely I have stilled and quieted myself as a weaned child beside his mother ....

Is David suggesting that our relationship to our Creator should be like that of a weaned child rather than that of a strident student constantly challenging his teacher? (Note, incidentally, the striking identity of phrases in David's things too wondrous for me — *nifla-ot mimeni,* and the words of Job in 42:2: "I have spoken ... of things too wondrous for me" — *nifla-ot mimeni.)* Habakkuk 2:20 echoes this: "The Lord is in His holy Temple; *hass mipanav* — be silent before Him, all the earth." The ultimate religious posture, that of abject surrender to the Creator, is here espoused. Thy will be done; no questions asked. Be silent before Him. As Job expresses it in 13:15, in the ultimate declaration of genuine faith: "Though He slay me, yet will I trust in Him ...."

And yet, an opposing facet of human life confronts us: our minds are finite and mortal, yes, but it is clear that God endowed us with inquiring minds that insist on answers and will not rest. When questions arise about the very nature of God's justice and righteousness, the human soul is not content with responses that offer only obeisance to mysteries beyond our knowledge. Such attitudes and such answers do not nourish the soul. Man will continue to ask, to probe, to seek to comprehend the incomprehensible and to fathom the unfathomable.

Particularly heart-rending is the question of "why" when posed by a suffering man or woman, or by a survivor of the Shoah. As we listen to the anguished cry of the sufferer, as we stand alongside him at the edge of the stark abyss, can we offer her only a frigid silence, and show him only the dark, mute wall of inability to understand? The scalding pain of devastating illness is not eased by philosophic meanderings about theodicy.

For while it is true, as the Talmud states in *Berachot* 5a, that God gave three significant gifts to the Jewish people — Torah, the Land of Israel, and the World-to-Come — and that these were each given through pain and suffering (*yisurin*); and while there exists the concept of *yisurin shel ahavah* — "afflictions of love," based on Proverbs 3:12, "Whom God loves, He chastises" — meaning, among other things, that if God had truly abandoned us He would not trouble to chastise us; and while it is true that this seems to suggest that anguish and suffering are apparently integral parts of the

Jewish condition, and that they are an inevitable and necessary component of the ultimate good — who would be brutal enough to share such thoughts with the grief-stricken mother?

Rather than to intellectualize and attempt to shrink the Infinite into our limited and constricted vessels of comprehension, it would be far more helpful and comforting if we were able to internalize the teachings of Psalm 92:3: "… to relate Your kindness in the morning, and Your faith at night." That is to say, it is in the night of the soul that one's faith and trust in the ineffable and concealed Creator must be encouraged to break out of its inner recesses within the soul and to shine forth — so the sufferer senses that at the very least the suffering has not been without purpose.

Clearly, there is no set formula that can be applied to all situations, because human suffering and tragedy are not formulaic. Every situation requires its own response. But suffusing it all must be the sense of God's overpowering care and love for His creatures, His Presence in every facet of life, and, as the Sages repeatedly emphasize, the fact that He suffers in His own ineffable way whenever His creatures suffer.

And so we end as we began. Why does the way of the wicked prosper? Why do the righteous suffer? Perhaps some day, in the fullness of time, our loving Creator will unravel for us the mysteries of life and death, good and evil, despair and redemption. But at the present moment it is not in our power to know the secrets of the Unknowable One above.

And so we all complete our lives as we began our lives. Not as innocently, perhaps, but just as uncomprehendingly — in the words of Proverbs, "as a weaned child beside his mother." But some glorious day, He Who watches over us from His hidden places will grant us the ability to comprehend the awesome answers to our awesome questions. And, if we are truly worthy of His love, He will grant us the wisdom to comprehend an even more profound truth: that our questions were not questions at all.